Deploying to OpenShift

A Guide for Busy Developers

Graham Dumpleton

Beijing · Boston · Farnham · Sebastopol · Tokyo

Deploying to OpenShift

by Graham Dumpleton

Published by O'Reilly Media, Inc., 1005 Gravenstein Highway North, Sebastopol, CA 95472.

O'Reilly books may be purchased for educational, business, or sales promotional use. Online editions are also available for most titles (*http://oreilly.com/safari*). For more information, contact our corporate/institutional sales department: 800-998-9938 or *corporate@oreilly.com*.

Editors: Virginia Wilson and Nikki McDonald	**Indexer:** Judy McConville
Production Editor: Melanie Yarbrough	**Interior Designer:** David Futato
Copyeditor: Dwight Ramsey	**Cover Designer:** Karen Montgomery
Proofreader: Rachel Head	**Illustrator:** Rebecca Demarest

April 2018:   First Edition

Revision History for the First Edition
2018-05-01:   First Release

This work is part of a collaboration between O'Reilly and Red Hat. See our *statement of editorial independence* (*http://www.oreilly.com/about/editorial_independence.html*).

978-1-491-95716-5

[LSI]

Table of Contents

Preface. ix

1. The OpenShift Container Platform. 1
   The Role of Containers   2
   Orchestrating at Scale   3
   Containers as a Service   4
   Platform as a Service   4
   Deploying Your Application   5

2. Running an OpenShift Cluster. 7
   Using OpenShift Online   7
   Installing OpenShift Origin   8
   Launching Using Minishift   8
   Running oc cluster up   10
   Summary   11

3. Accessing the OpenShift Cluster. 13
   Using the Web Console   13
   Using the Command Line   14
   Using the OpenShift REST API   17
   Summary   18

4. Adding Applications to a Project. 19
   The Role of a Project   19
   Creating a Project   20
   Adding a Collaborator   22
   Deploying Applications   23
   Deploying from the Catalog   24

Deploying an Image   26
Deploying a Set of Resources   27
Summary   28

5. Deploying Applications from Images. **29**
Deploying Your First Image   29
Scaling Up the Application   33
Runtime Configuration   33
Deleting the Application   34
Deploying Using the Web Console   34
Importing an Image   36
Pushing to the Registry   37
Images and Security   38
Summary   38

6. Building and Deploying from Source. **41**
The Source Build Strategy   42
Deploying from Source   42
Creating a Separate Build   44
Triggering a New Build   45
Building from a Local Source   46
Binary Input Builds   46
Testing the Container Image   47
Build and Runtime Configuration   48
Summary   49

7. Building an Image from a Dockerfile. **51**
The Docker Build Strategy   51
Security and Docker Builds   52
Creating the Build   52
Deploying the Image   53
Build and Runtime Configuration   53
Using an Inline Dockerfile   55
Summary   56

8. Understanding Source-to-Image Builders. **57**
The Source-to-Image Project   57
Building the Application Image   58
Assembling the Source Code   59
Creating an S2I Builder Image   60
Building the S2I Builder Image   62
Using the S2I Builder with OpenShift   62

Adding an S2I Builder to the Catalog   63
Summary   64

9. Customizing Source-to-Image Builds... 65
Using Environment Variables   65
Overriding the Builder Scripts   66
Read-Only Code Repositories   68
Overriding the Runtime Image   68
Updating the Image Metadata   69
Summary   71

10. Using Incremental and Chained Builds... 73
Faster Builds Using Caching   73
Using Incremental Builds   74
Saving Artifacts from a Build   75
Restoring the Build Artifacts   75
Enabling Incremental Builds   76
Using Chained Builds   77
Summary   78

11. Webhooks and Build Automation.. 79
Using a Hosted Git Repository   79
Accessing a Private Git Repository   80
Adding a Repository Webhook   82
Customized Build Triggers   83
Summary   83

12. Configuration and Secrets... 85
Passing Environment Variables   85
Working with Configuration Files   87
Handling of Secret Information   89
Deleting Configuration and Secrets   91
Summary   92

13. Services, Networking, and Routing... 93
Containers and Pods   93
Services and Endpoints   94
Connecting Between Projects   96
Creating External Routes   96
Using Secure Connections   98
Internal and External Ports   99
Exposing Non-HTTP Services   100

Local Port Forwarding   100
Summary   101

14. Working with Persistent Storage. **103**
Types of Persistent Storage   103
Claiming a Persistent Volume   105
Unmounting a Persistent Volume   106
Reusing a Persistent Volume Claim   106
Sharing Between Applications   106
Sharing Between Containers   107
Deleting a Persistent Volume   107
Copying Data to a Volume   108
Summary   108

15. Resource Quotas and Limits. **109**
What Is Managed by Quotas   109
Quotas versus Limit Ranges   111
Requests Versus Limits   112
Resource Requirements   113
Overriding Build Resources   114
Summary   114

16. Monitoring Application Health. **115**
The Role of a Readiness Probe   115
The Role of a Liveness Probe   116
Using an HTTP Request   116
Using a Container Command   117
Using a Socket Connection   118
Probe Frequency and Timeouts   118
Summary   120

17. Application Lifecycle Management. **121**
Deployment Strategies   121
Rolling Deployment   122
Recreate Deployment   123
Custom Deployments   124
Container Runtime Hooks   125
Init Containers   126
Summary   127

18. Logging, Monitoring, and Debugging. **129**
Viewing the Build Logs   129

Viewing Application Logs   130
Monitoring Resource Objects   131
Monitoring System Events   132
Viewing Container Metrics   132
Running an Interactive Shell   133
Debugging Startup Failures   133
Summary   134

Afterword. **137**

Index. **139**

Preface

OpenShift implements a polyglot platform for the deployment of web applications and services. It uses containers in conjunction with a Security-Enhanced Linux (SELinux) environment to implement a secure multitenant environment suitable for the enterprise. You can deploy OpenShift in your own infrastructure or on public clouds, or you can use OpenShift Online, Red Hat's cloud-based hosting service.

The latest version of OpenShift uses the industry-standard Kubernetes platform from the Cloud Native Computing Foundation (CNCF) (*https://www.cncf.io*) for managing and running applications within containers at scale. The ability to run any application image is ensured through adherence to image and runtime specifications from the Open Container Initiative (OCI) (*https://www.opencontainers.org*).

OpenShift offers you the ability to easily deploy your web application code directly using a library of predefined image builders, or you can bring your own container images. With support in OpenShift for features such as persistent volumes, you are not limited to just running stateless 12-factor or cloud-native applications. Using OpenShift, you can also deploy databases and many legacy applications that you otherwise would not be able to run on a traditional Platform as a Service (PaaS) offering.

OpenShift is a complete container application platform. It is a modern take on the traditional PaaS that you can use with your existing applications, but that also provides the power and flexibility to meet future needs.

Who Should Read This Book

This book is intended for developers who are evaluating OpenShift, or have already decided to use it, and who seek a more in-depth knowledge of the core features of OpenShift that are used to deploy applications. It will also be of interest to administrators who are managing an OpenShift cluster and who need to provide assistance to developers using the platform.

The book is the third in a series of books from Red Hat about the latest version of OpenShift. The prior books in the series are:

- *OpenShift for Developers: A Guide for Impatient Beginners* (*https://www.open shift.com/promotions/for-developers.html*)
- *DevOps with OpenShift: Cloud Deployments Made Easy* (*https://www.open shift.com/promotions/devops-with-openshift.html*)

Why I Wrote This Book

The first book, *OpenShift for Developers*, which I coauthored with Grant Shipley, aimed to get you started as quickly as possible by skipping many of the details. Those details are important, though, when you want to make the most of OpenShift. In this book I wanted to fill in some of those gaps to give you that broader understanding of OpenShift and how it can make your job of deploying applications to the cloud easier.

The topics I have chosen for the book are based on my experience of having to answer many a question on public community forums (such as Stack Overflow and Google Groups) and at conferences, in my role at Red Hat working as a Developer Advocate for OpenShift.

The aim is that this book will act as a quick reference guide you can keep coming back to in order to refresh your memory on commonly used patterns, or to learn more about additional topics as you continue to use OpenShift.

Online Resources

As with many new technologies, OpenShift is still evolving as it adapts to the wide range of use cases it is applied to. When you come to read this book, some information may not provide the most up-to-date picture. That's why we encourage you to check online resources for the latest details on OpenShift and how to use it.

The OpenShift documentation (*https://docs.openshift.com/*) is a great place to start when you're looking for information about OpenShift, from OpenShift Online to Red Hat's enterprise products.

To learn more about OpenShift by working through online training exercises, you can use the interactive learning portal (*https://learn.openshift.com/*) for OpenShift, implemented on top of Katacoda (*https://katacoda.com/*).

To run OpenShift Origin locally on your own computer in a virtual machine, you can use Minishift (*https://www.openshift.org/minishift/*).

If you are interested in the source code for OpenShift, it is available via the OpenShift Origin (*https://github.com/openshift/*) project.

OpenShift Origin is the upstream open source project that is used to create the Red Hat OpenShift product range. OpenShift Origin will always include all the latest features, including experimental features, with support being provided by the OpenShift community. You are warmly invited to clone the OpenShift Origin project code, send in your contributions, or open an issue to report any problems you find.

The OpenShift product releases are created as regular snapshots of the OpenShift Origin project. The product releases do not always have the very latest features enabled, but if you have a commercial Red Hat subscription, the product releases include support from Red Hat.

If you would like to try out the OpenShift enterprise products, a number of options are available.

The first is to sign up to the Red Hat Developers Program (*https://develop ers.redhat.com/*). This is a free program and allows you to access versions of Red Hat products for personal use on your own computer. One of the products made available through the program is the Red Hat Container Development Kit (*http://red.ht/ 2FrWpHC*). This includes a version of OpenShift that you can run inside a virtual machine on your own computer, but which is based on the OpenShift Container Platform (*http://red.ht/2FsRtT6*) product rather than OpenShift Origin.

A second way of trying out OpenShift Container Platform is via a free test drive (*http://red.ht/2FrvKec*) with the leading cloud service providers. This will set you up an OpenShift environment running across a multinode cluster on the cloud provider of your choice.

Like what you see and just want to get your website out there and being used, without needing to set up and run your own OpenShift cluster? Check out OpenShift Online (*https://www.openshift.com/get-started/*), Red Hat's public cloud-based hosting service.

Want to hear about how others in the OpenShift community are using OpenShift, or wish to share your own experiences? You can join OpenShift Commons (*https:// commons.openshift.org*).

In addition to hearing from OpenShift community members, also check out the OpenShift blog (*https://blog.openshift.com*), where regular articles from members of the OpenShift team at Red Hat are published.

If you have questions about the development of OpenShift, you can reach the OpenShift development team through the OpenShift mailing lists (*http://red.ht/2FplfIu*), or in the #openshift-dev channel on IRC's Freenode network. Community support for OpenShift Online can be found on Google Groups (*http://bit.ly/2FtUnXS*) or Stack Overflow (*https://stackoverflow.com*).

Conventions Used in This Book

The following typographical conventions are used in this book:

Italic

Indicates new terms, URLs, email addresses, filenames, and file extensions.

`Constant width`

Used for program listings, as well as within paragraphs to refer to program elements such as variable or function names, databases, data types, environment variables, statements, and keywords.

`Constant width bold`

Shows commands or other text that should be typed literally by the user.

`Constant width italic`

Shows text that should be replaced with user-supplied values or by values determined by context.

This element signifies a tip or suggestion.

This element indicates a warning or caution.

O'Reilly Safari

 *Safari* (formerly Safari Books Online) is a membership-based training and reference platform for enterprise, government, educators, and individuals.

Members have access to thousands of books, training videos, Learning Paths, interactive tutorials, and curated playlists from over 250 publishers, including O'Reilly Media, Harvard Business Review, Prentice Hall Professional, Addison-Wesley Professional, Microsoft Press, Sams, Que, Peachpit Press, Adobe, Focal Press, Cisco Press, John Wiley & Sons, Syngress, Morgan Kaufmann, IBM Redbooks, Packt, Adobe Press, FT Press, Apress, Manning, New Riders, McGraw-Hill, Jones & Bartlett, and Course Technology, among others.

For more information, please visit *http://oreilly.com/safari*.

How to Contact Us

Please address comments and questions concerning this book to the publisher:

O'Reilly Media, Inc.
1005 Gravenstein Highway North
Sebastopol, CA 95472
800-998-9938 (in the United States or Canada)
707-829-0515 (international or local)
707-829-0104 (fax)

We have a web page for this book, where we list errata, examples, and any additional information. You can access this page at *http://bit.ly/deploying-to-open-shift*.

To comment or ask technical questions about this book, send email to *bookquestions@oreilly.com*.

For more information about our books, courses, conferences, and news, see our website at *http://www.oreilly.com*.

Find us on Facebook: *http://facebook.com/oreilly*

Follow us on Twitter: *http://twitter.com/oreillymedia*

Watch us on YouTube: *http://www.youtube.com/oreillymedia*

Acknowledgments

This book has been a long time in the making, with it being put aside a number of times as work and other life events intruded. Through all that time my wife, Wendy, and children, Kara and Caiden, have continued to put up with me never seeming to ever leave my home office. My children would wait patiently, although never patiently enough, for the end of the week to come, when I would emerge from my office and we would spend a good amount of time together over the weekend playing Minecraft. With this book complete, I know they will be looking forward to the additional time I will now be able to spend with them.

I would also like to thank the other members of the OpenShift evangelist team at Red Hat with whom I work and who tolerate my grumpiness, especially when I can't seem to get OpenShift doing what I want it to do. Special thanks go to Jorge Morales, who is always there when I need help in understanding how something works, or need a sounding board for one of my crazy ideas. Jorge also provided valuable feedback on this book. Luckily my Aussie accent doesn't come through in my writing, as even after two years of working with Jorge, when I speak he still often doesn't have a clue what I am saying.

## CHAPTER 1

The OpenShift Container Platform

The OpenShift platform was launched in May 2011. The source code was made available through an open source project, with anyone being able to download it and use it. Red Hat also offered a supported version of OpenShift for use in enterprise deployments, and a hosted service called OpenShift Online.

OpenShift has always been implemented on top of containers, but technology is always evolving. In June 2013 a major rewrite began to reimplement OpenShift on top of the latest evolving technologies in the container space. Version 1.0 of OpenShift Origin, based around Kubernetes (*https://kubernetes.io*) and the Docker container runtime, was released in June 2015. At the time of writing this book OpenShift 3.6 was the latest version, with the 3.7 release imminent and new releases coming out on a quarterly basis.

What exactly is OpenShift, though?

In simple terms, it is a platform to help you develop and then deploy applications to one or more hosts. These can be public-facing web applications, or backend applications including microservices or databases. Applications can be implemented in any programming language you choose. The only requirement is that the application can run within a container.

OpenShift can run anywhere you can run Red Hat Enterprise Linux (RHEL), CentOS, or Fedora. This can be on public or private cloud infrastructure, directly on physical hardware, or using virtual machines.

In this initial chapter you will learn more about the technologies that OpenShift uses, and where it fits within the cloud computing ecosystem.

The Role of Containers

The National Institute of Standards and Technology (NIST) defines as part of their definition of cloud computing (*http://bit.ly/2GLLcPu*) three standard service models for the provision of cloud computing services:

Software as a Service (SaaS)
> The capability provided to the consumer is to use the provider's applications running on a cloud infrastructure. The applications are accessible from various client devices through either a thin client interface, such as a web browser (e.g., web-based email), or a program interface. The consumer does not manage or control the underlying cloud infrastructure including network, servers, operating systems, storage, or even individual application capabilities, with the possible exception of limited user-specific application configuration settings.

Platform as a Service (PaaS)
> The capability provided to the consumer is to deploy onto the cloud infrastructure consumer-created or acquired applications created using programming languages, libraries, services, and tools supported by the provider. The consumer does not manage or control the underlying cloud infrastructure including network, servers, operating systems, or storage, but has control over the deployed applications and possibly configuration settings for the application-hosting environment.

Infrastructure as a Service (IaaS)
> The capability provided to the consumer is to provision processing, storage, networks, and other fundamental computing resources where the consumer is able to deploy and run arbitrary software, which can include operating systems and applications. The consumer does not manage or control the underlying cloud infrastructure but has control over operating systems, storage, and deployed applications; and possibly limited control of select networking components (e.g., host firewalls).

Under these traditional definitions for cloud service computing models, OpenShift would be classified a PaaS. In both PaaS and SaaS models, containerization is often used for separating applications from each other and from different users.

Containers as a technology have a long history, with forerunners being FreeBSD jails and Solaris Zones. In Linux, support for containers revolves around the Linux Containers project (LXC). This brought user-space tooling on top of Linux kernel features such as cgroups and namespaces, with security additions from Seccomp and SELinux. The LXC tools made the use of containers in Linux accessible, but it could still be a fiddly process to set up and run applications in containers.

In 2013 a company called dotCloud, a PaaS provider, announced in a lightning talk at PyCon US a tool called Docker. This tool was an outgrowth of the proprietary technology that dotCloud used to help run applications in containers; it provided a wrapper for making it easier to launch applications in containers using LXC.

The Docker tool was quickly picked up by developers as it addressed two key issues. The first was a definition of a common packaging format for an image, which contained an application and all the dependencies it required, including operating system libraries and programs. The second was tooling for building this image.

These together made it possible to create application images that could be easily moved between different systems, to then be run in a container, with higher confidence that they would work out of the box.

The technology around the Docker tool was split out separately from the company dotCloud and a new company, Docker Inc., was created to manage development of the technology. Because of the growing interest in the technology, the Open Containers Initiative (OCI) was later formed to provide an open governance structure for the express purpose of creating open industry standards around the container format and runtime. This process was seeded with specifications derived from the Docker tool. OCI currently acts as the steward for two specifications: the Runtime Specification (runtime-spec) and the Image Specification (image-spec).

Orchestrating at Scale

The Docker tool made it easier for developers to build application images and run a single application in a container on a single host. But scaling up an application to have multiple instances running on the same host, or across multiple hosts, required additional software components to help orchestrate the deployment and running of the application, as well as a router to load-balance traffic to each instance of the application.

During the initial phase of Docker adoption, no out-of-the-box solutions existed for the orchestration and routing layer, which resulted in users handcrafting homegrown solutions.

In mid-2014, Google announced the Kubernetes project, an open source system for automating deployment, scaling, and management of containerized applications. This provided one of the missing components required in trying to handle running containers at scale.

At the time, Red Hat was already well into a project to reimplement OpenShift around Docker but had been implementing its own orchestration layer. With the announcement of Kubernetes, Red Hat decided to drop its own efforts, adopting Kubernetes and becoming a major contributor to the project.

Kubernetes was subsequently released as 1.0 in July 2015, with the project being donated to the Cloud Native Computing Foundation (CNCF). It has since become the de facto standard for container orchestration.

Containers as a Service

Kubernetes does not fit any of the existing service model classifications for cloud computing. This has resulted in the new name, Containers as a Service (CaaS), being coined. This service model can be seen as similar to IaaS, except that instead of being provided with a virtual machine, you are provided with a container. Figure 1-1 shows where CaaS fits in among the other service models.

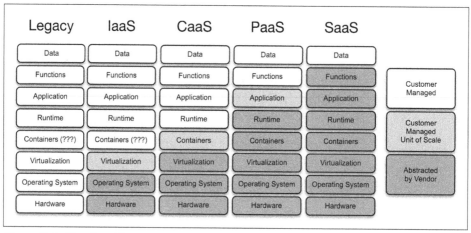

Figure 1-1. Cloud services

To run your application in a CaaS, you need to provide the application image you have built, which contains your application and any operating system libraries and programs you require. Although an application image contains a copy of these operating system libraries and programs, it is only your application process that is run.

Platform as a Service

Using the CaaS capability of Kubernetes, OpenShift is able to deploy an application from a container image stored in any image registry. Kubernetes alone does not provide any support for building the container image. You need to run a build tool to create your application image on a separate system and push that to an image registry from which it can be deployed. This is because a CaaS focuses on just running containers and lacks the capability of a PaaS, where you can provide your source code and the platform will work out how to get that running in a container.

To provide the PaaS capability of being able to take source code and deploy it, Open-Shift adds automation for performing builds on top of Kubernetes. OpenShift supports two main strategies for building from source code.

In the style of a traditional PaaS, OpenShift can take your application source code and, using a builder for the programming language you are using, create your application image. You as a developer do not need to provide instructions on how to create the container image; the platform will do this for you.

In addition, OpenShift can also accept source code that includes a set of instructions to create the application image in a *Dockerfile*. This is what you need to do if building a container image yourself using Docker, but OpenShift will do it for you, inside the OpenShift platform.

In both cases, OpenShift will cache the application image in an image registry that it provides. The application image will then be deployed from this internal image registry.

Using OpenShift to build the application image from a *Dockerfile* means you do not need to have the Docker tool on your own system, nor do you need to use a separate image registry to hold your images.

With both types of builds, OpenShift can pull the source code for the build from a hosted Git repository. If you're using a service such as GitHub, GitLab, or Bitbucket, you can configure the Git repository hosting service to notify OpenShift whenever you push changes to your code back to the hosted Git repository. This notification can trigger a new build and deployment of your application.

This automation means that once you have set up your application in OpenShift, you do not need to interact directly with OpenShift as you continue with your application development. As soon as you push back changes to your hosted Git repository, Open-Shift will know and can build and redeploy the application automatically.

Deploying Your Application

By building on top of Kubernetes, adding its own automation for builds and deployments, OpenShift operates as both a CaaS and a PaaS. In other words, OpenShift implements a general-purpose container platform. You can deploy your own bespoke applications, or you can import third-party applications such as databases, messaging systems, or other business suites to support the business processes of your organization.

In this book you will learn about the different ways you can deploy applications to OpenShift. This will include deploying from a prebuilt application image using the CaaS functionality of OpenShift, and building from source code in the manner of a PaaS.

You will also learn how to integrate your application into the OpenShift platform, how to configure it through OpenShift, how to mount persistent volumes, how to make it public so users can access it, and how to monitor and debug your application.

To interact with OpenShift you can use either a web console or a command-line client. This book will focus on using the command-line client.

The main application example that will be used throughout the book is a Python application implemented using the Django web framework. This is the same sample application that is used in many of the tutorials found on the OpenShift Interactive Learning Portal (*https://learn.openshift.com*). In addition to reading through this book, you can use those tutorials to further investigate many of the topics we cover.

The source code for the sample application can be found on GitHub (*https://github.com/openshift-katacoda/blog-django-py*).

If you wish to work through the example in the book yourself, you can use the playground environments on the OpenShift Interactive Learning Portal. The playgrounds don't follow a set tutorial, and you are free to try anything you want.

You can also install OpenShift yourself, or use a hosted OpenShift service. The next chapter will discuss options for running OpenShift, with the remainder of the book then showing you how to use it so you can learn to deploy your own applications.

## CHAPTER 2

Running an OpenShift Cluster

The easiest way to get started with OpenShift is to get access to a hosted version, such as OpenShift Online from Red Hat.

To install and run OpenShift yourself, you can download the source from the upstream OpenShift Origin project.

For quickly running OpenShift on your own computer, you can launch a prebuilt version of OpenShift.

In this chapter you will learn about these different options, including additional details on how you can get OpenShift running locally using Minishift and `oc cluster up`.

Using OpenShift Online

OpenShift Online (*https://www.openshift.com/get-started/*) is Red Hat's publicly hosted OpenShift service. If you do not want to install and manage your own OpenShift cluster, this is the option for you.

OpenShift Online provides a free starter tier, intended for experimentation, testing, or development. When you are ready to move your application to production and make it available to others to use, or you need additional resources beyond those provided by the free tier, you can upgrade to the paid tier.

Outgrown OpenShift Online, but still do not want to install and manage OpenShift yourself? Red Hat also offers OpenShift Dedicated (*https://www.openshift.com/dedicated/*). This service is similar to OpenShift Online, but the OpenShift cluster is reserved for your use and is not shared by other users outside your organization.

Installing OpenShift Origin

If you prefer to install and run OpenShift yourself, you can install OpenShift Origin (*https://www.openshift.org/*). The recommended installation method for OpenShift Origin uses a set of Ansible playbooks. Provide details about your environment and the machine nodes you have available, run Ansible, and the cluster will be set up for you.

Configuring and installing an OpenShift cluster from scratch is not something that will be covered in this book. You can find instructions in the Advanced Installation documentation (*http://bit.ly/2H3KHjC*) on the OpenShift Origin website.

OpenShift Origin is a community-supported distribution of OpenShift. If you would prefer to run your own OpenShift cluster but have access to professional support services, you can obtain a subscription for OpenShift Container Platform (*https://www.openshift.com/container-platform/*) from Red Hat.

Launching Using Minishift

For quickly starting up an OpenShift cluster locally, an alternative to building a cluster using OpenShift Origin is to start up a prebuilt system inside a virtual machine (VM).

To start OpenShift inside a VM, you can use Minishift (*https://www.openshift.org/minishift/*). This isn't an OpenShift distribution in itself, but a tool that you can run to create a minimal VM that includes a container service. Minishift then uses the OpenShift client oc to start up an OpenShift cluster by downloading and launching a preformatted container image containing OpenShift.

Running Minishift requires a hypervisor to run the VM containing OpenShift. Depending on your host operating system, you have the choice of the following hypervisors:

- macOS: xhyve (default), VirtualBox
- GNU/Linux: KVM (default), VirtualBox
- Windows: Hyper-V (default), VirtualBox

To download the latest Minishift release and view any release notes, visit the Minishift releases page (*https://github.com/minishift/minishift/releases*). If using macOS, you can also install Minishift using Homebrew (*https://brew.sh*). Before using Minishift, ensure you check out the installation instructions (*https://docs.openshift.org/latest/minishift/getting-started/index.html*) for any prerequisites your system must satisfy.

With the Minishift program installed, you can begin installation and start up the OpenShift cluster by running the minishift start command:

```
$ minishift start
Starting local OpenShift cluster using 'kvm' hypervisor...
...
    OpenShift server started.
    The server is accessible via web console at:
        https://192.168.99.128:8443

    You are logged in as:
        User:     developer
        Password: developer

    To login as administrator:
        oc login -u system:admin
```

By default Minishift attempts to use the virtualization driver native to the operating system. To use a different driver, set the --vm-driver flag when running this command. For example, to use VirtualBox, run minishift start --vm-driver=virtualbox. For more information about the available options, run minishift start --help.

When Minishift is first run, it will automatically download and install the OpenShift oc client binary specific to your operating system. This will be installed in a *cache* directory in your home directory, keyed by the version of OpenShift being run. Run the command minishift oc-env to output instructions on how to set up your shell environment so it can find the oc program:

```
$ minishift oc-env
export PATH="/Users/graham/.minishift/cache/oc/v1.5.0:$PATH"
# Run this command to configure your shell:
# eval $(minishift oc-env)
```

To access the web console for OpenShift, run the command minishift console. This will open up a browser client for you in the web console.

To determine the URL for the OpenShift cluster, for use when logging in from the command line or accessing the web console from a browser, run the command minishift console --url. The login credentials you should use with the OpenShift cluster created by Minishift are:

- Username: developer
- Password: developer

To shut down the OpenShift cluster, run the command minishift stop. You can restart it again using minishift start. All your work will be restored on a restart. To delete the OpenShift cluster, run the command minishift delete.

When Minishift creates a cluster, it will use default settings for the number of CPUs, memory available, and the size of the VM disk. It is recommended you override these with values that better match what resources you have available, or need. This can be done using options to `minishift start` the first time it is used to create the Open-Shift cluster. You can override the default values for these resources, as well as the VM driver used, using the `minishift config` command.

 Minishift uses OpenShift Origin. For a version of Minishift that uses OpenShift Container Platform from Red Hat, see the Red Hat Container Development Kit (*https://developers.redhat.com/prod ucts/cdk/overview/*).

Running oc cluster up

The main feature that Minishift provides is the creation of a virtual machine. For the setup and starting of the OpenShift cluster within that VM, Minishift delegates control to the command `oc cluster up`.

The `oc` program is the standard command-line client for OpenShift. If you already have a local container service running on your computer, instead of using Minishift and running OpenShift inside a VM, you can run it with the container service instance you already have.

You can download an archive file containing the `oc` program for your operating system from the releases page (*https://github.com/openshift/origin/releases*) for Open-Shift Origin.

Before running `oc cluster up`, ensure you check the installation instructions (*https://github.com/openshift/origin/blob/master/docs/cluster_up_down.md*) as there are a number of prerequisite steps you must perform to configure your local system.

When you're ready, to start OpenShift, run the command:

```
$ oc cluster up
-- Checking OpenShift client ... OK
-- Checking Docker client ... OK
-- Checking Docker version ... OK
-- Checking for existing OpenShift container ... OK
-- Checking for openshift/origin:v1.5.0 image ...
   Pulling image openshift/origin:v1.5.0
....
-- Server Information ...
   OpenShift server started.
   The server is accessible via web console at:
       https://127.0.0.1:8443

   You are logged in as:
```

```
User:     developer
Password: developer

To login as administrator:
   oc login -u system:admin
```

To find the URL for the OpenShift web console, you can run oc whoami --show-server. To shut down the OpenShift cluster, run oc cluster down.

The oc cluster up command is intended for local development and testing, not for production use.

By default, when you run oc cluster up, anything you do within the OpenShift cluster is not persistent. That is, when you run oc cluster down, you will lose all your work.

In order for your work to be saved, you must supply additional command-line options to oc cluster up. The same options must be supplied when restarting it after a shutdown:

```
$ oc cluster up --use-existing-config \
  --host-config-dir $HOME/.oc-cluster-up/config \
  --host-data-dir $HOME/.oc-cluster-up/data
```

Run oc cluster up --help to find out what options are available, and see the installation instructions for further information on their use.

Summary

You can install OpenShift in numerous ways—direct to a physical machine, on a virtual machine, or in a private or public cloud. OpenShift would normally be installed across a cluster of machines to provide the capability to run applications at scale.

Even if you are using a separate managed OpenShift environment, as a developer, it is still a good idea to install Minishift on your own local machine. A local installation of Minishift can be used to experiment with OpenShift or to try out a newer version. You could also integrate Minishift into your development process, working on your application locally before migrating the code, or an application image, into your production environment.

If you only want to experiment with OpenShift, a playground can be created on the OpenShift Interactive Learning Portal (*https://learn.openshift.com*). This will provide you with a temporary environment you can use through your browser, without needing to install anything on your local machine.

## CHAPTER 3

Accessing the OpenShift Cluster

At this point, you should have a basic understanding of the OpenShift platform and what it can be used for. To deploy your own applications to an OpenShift cluster, you can use either the OpenShift web console, or the `oc` command-line client.

Before you can do anything, though, you first need to log in to the OpenShift cluster. As OpenShift is a multitenant environment you will use your own account.

If you have installed Minishift or run `oc cluster up` on your own computer, an account is preconfigured for you. The username of that account will be `developer`. Minishift and `oc cluster up` will accept any value for a password. If you log in with a different username, it will automatically configure a new account.

If you are using a hosted OpenShift environment, such as OpenShift Online, the login credentials will be what you signed up to the service with, or you may need to log in with a third-party identity provider.

This chapter will describe how to log in to OpenShift through the web console and `oc` command-line client. It will also explain how you can retrieve an access token for your active login session, which can be used to access the OpenShift cluster when using the REST API.

Using the Web Console

The easiest way to access and interact with OpenShift is through the web console. The URL for the web console will be dictated by what was specified as the public URL for the OpenShift cluster. Once the console is accessed, how you then log in will depend on the configured identity provider.

In the simple case, the web console login page will ask you for your username and password, as shown in Figure 3-1.

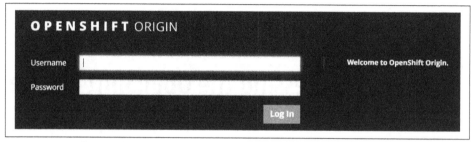

Figure 3-1. Web console login

In the case of an external OpenID Connect or OAuth authentication service provider being used, it will be necessary to log in through the external service (Figure 3-2).

Figure 3-2. Web console login via Red Hat

For a new user, once you have logged in, you should be presented with the "Welcome to OpenShift" screen and the option of creating a new project (Figure 3-3).

Figure 3-3. Web console welcome

Using the Command Line

The web console provides a convenient method for quickly interacting with and viewing the state of applications you have deployed using OpenShift. But not everything you may want to do, especially in a cluster or project administrator role, can be done through the web console. You will therefore also need to be familiar with using the OpenShift command-line tool, oc.

Always use a version of the oc command-line tool that matches the version of the OpenShift environment you are using. If you use an older version of the oc command-line client, you will not have access to all the features of the newer version of OpenShift.

This will obviously be the case where the feature is dependent on a new command type or command-line option implemented in the oc command-line tool. When using an older client, you can also be restricted in your ability to make queries about new types of resource objects implemented by OpenShift.

If you do not already have the oc command-line tool, you can download the version corresponding to the OpenShift cluster you are using from the web console by following the steps in Figure 3-4. The same page also provides you with the command you need to run to log in.

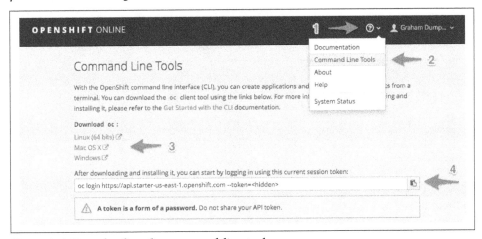

Figure 3-4. Downloading the command-line tool

❶   Select the "?" drop-down menu from the navigation bar.

❷   Select the Command Line Tools menu option.

❸   Select the download link for your platform.

❹   Click the copy icon to capture the login command, including the login token, then paste it into your terminal window and run it.

The form of the login command, with the token, is:

```
oc login https://api.starter-us-east-1.openshift.com --token=Sbqw....T3UU
```

The token used when you log in will periodically expire, and you will need to log in again when it does. When this occurs, you can run `oc login` with no options:

```
$ oc login
Login failed (401 Unauthorized)
You must obtain an API token by visiting
   https://api.starter-us-east-1.openshift.com/oauth/token/request
```

This will direct you to an alternate page, shown in Figure 3-5, where you can obtain a new token.

Figure 3-5. Obtaining a new access token

Utilizing an access token when logging in from the command line is the preferred mechanism as it ensures that sessions will be expired periodically. When an OpenShift cluster is not using an external identity provider, it may also allow login from the command line using a username and password. If this is the case, running `oc login` with no options will prompt you for your credentials:

```
$ oc login
Authentication required for https://127.0.0.1:8443 (openshift)
Username: developer
Password:
Login successful.

You don't have any projects. You can try to create a new project, by running
```

```
oc new-project <projectname>
```

For help on the specific options accepted by oc login, or any other command, run the command but with the --help option:

```
$ oc login --help
```

To get general information about the oc command, run it with no options.

To get a list of all the commands that oc accepts, run it with the help command:

```
$ oc help
```

For details on common options accepted by all commands, run it with the options command:

```
$ oc options
```

Many commands will accept --dry-run as an option. This can be used to validate that the combination of options you passed the command were correct, without making any changes.

Using the OpenShift REST API

When you use the web console or oc command-line tool, it communicates with OpenShift using a REST API endpoint. You can also access this REST API directly using a simple HTTP client, or by using a custom client for a specific programming language generated from the Swagger API specification for OpenShift.

The same access token used when logging in from the command line can be used when making an HTTP call against the REST API. This token should be included as part of the value for the Authorization header sent with the HTTP request.

An example of a curl command for requesting your user details via the REST API was given in the page displayed for obtaining a new token (Figure 3-5):

```
curl -H "Authorization: Bearer 1CFH...ND5o" \
    "https://api.starter-us-east-1.openshift.com/oapi/v1/users/~"
```

If you are already logged in from the command line and need the token, you can also obtain it by running the oc whoami --show-token command. This command could be used in a script to obtain the token prior to making a request:

```
#!/bin/sh

SERVER=`oc whoami --show-server`
TOKEN=`oc whoami --show-token`

URL="$SERVER/oapi/v1/users/~"
```

```
curl -H "Authorization: Bearer $TOKEN" $URL
```

As when logging in using oc login, this token will expire and will need to be renewed.

The REST API can be used to manage end-user applications, the cluster, and the users of the cluster. This book will not delve into how to use the REST API; for further information, see the OpenShift REST API documentation (*https://docs.open shift.org/latest/rest_api/index.html*).

One further option for learning how the REST API can be used is to look at what the oc command-line tool does when you use it. To see what REST API calls the oc client tool makes in order to execute a command, run the command and pass --loglevel 9 as an option. This will show verbose messages about what oc is doing, including the details and contents of the REST API calls.

Summary

All access to OpenShift is via the REST API. You can interact directly with the REST API if you need to create your own tools to control or work with OpenShift, but normally you would use the web console or oc command-line tool. If you are a developer, especially a power user, you will predominantly use the command line.

When working with OpenShift using the command line, you can operate at two levels. You can create or edit raw resource definitions in OpenShift to control how an application is deployed, or you can use commands and options implemented by the oc command-line tool to make changes for you.

In this book the focus will be on using oc and the commands and options it provides. This is a simpler path to using the capabilities of OpenShift and Kubernetes than working with raw resource definitions.

## CHAPTER 4

Adding Applications to a Project

Now that you know how to access your OpenShift cluster and can log in, you are almost ready to start deploying your first application.

Applications can be deployed from an existing container image that you have built outside the OpenShift cluster, or one that is supplied by a third party.

Or, if you have the source code for the application, you can have OpenShift build the image for you. OpenShift can build an image from instructions provided by a `Docker file`, or the source code can be run through a Source-to-Image (S2I) builder to produce the container image.

OpenShift also includes ready-to-run container images for popular database products such as PostgreSQL, MySQL, MongoDB, and Redis.

Before you can deploy any application, though, you first need to create a project in the OpenShift cluster to contain your applications.

In this chapter you will learn what projects are used for and how to create them. You will be provided with a quick tour of how you can find out what ready-to-run container images OpenShift provides, what languages are supported through the S2I builders, and the methods for deploying an application from an image or a set of resource definitions.

The Role of a Project

Whenever you work with OpenShift, you will work within the context of a project. This is a walled namespace used to hold everything related to a set of applications.

When you create a project, it is owned by you and you are the administrator for that project. Any application you deploy within the project is only visible to other applications running in the same project, unless you choose to make it public outside the OpenShift cluster.

You can deploy more than one application into a single project. You would usually do this if they have tight coupling. Or, you could instead choose to always create a separate project for each application and selectively set up access between projects if they needed to communicate with each other.

Creating a Project

When you access an OpenShift cluster for the first time, you will need to create a project. An exception to this is when you are using Minishift or `oc cluster up`. Because these are intended for local testing and development, for convenience they will set up an initial project for you.

If you use the web console to access the OpenShift cluster and there aren't any projects, you will be presented with the option to add a new project (see Figure 4-1).

Figure 4-1. Adding a project

Clicking New Project will bring up the form in Figure 4-2. Enter the name of the project and optionally provide a display name and description.

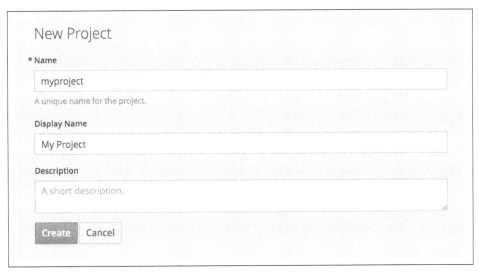

Figure 4-2. Creating a new project

When you specify a name for a project, it will need to satisfy a couple of requirements.

The first requirement is that the name you choose must be unique across the whole OpenShift cluster. This means you cannot use a project name that is already in use by another user.

The second requirement is that the name can only include lowercase letters, numbers, and the dash character. This is necessary as the project name is used as a component in the hostname assigned to an application when it is made visible outside the OpenShift cluster.

Once you have created a project and are on the Overview_ page, you can jump back to the project list (Figure 4-3) by clicking on the Home icon.

Figure 4-3. Project list

You can also jump between projects using the Projects drop-down menu in the top banner of any project.

Projects can be created from the command line too, by using the oc new-project command:

```
$ oc new-project myproject --display-name 'My Project'
Already on project "myproject" on server "https://localhost:8443".

You can add applications to this project with the 'new-app' command.
For example, try:

    oc new-app centos/ruby-22-centos7~https://github.com/openshift/ruby-ex.git

to build a new example application in Ruby.
```

You can list all projects you have access to using the oc projects command:

```
$ oc projects
You have one project on this server: "My Project (myproject)".

Using project "myproject" on server "https://localhost:8443".
```

The name of the current project, against which your commands will be applied, can be determined by running the command oc project:

```
$ oc project
Using project "myproject" on server "https://localhost:8443".
```

When you have access to multiple projects, you can set the current project by running oc project and specifying the name of the project:

```
$ oc project myproject
Now using project "myproject" on server "https://localhost:8443".
```

When you create a new project using oc new-project, the new project will automatically be set as the current project.

If you need to run a single command against a different project, you can pass the name of the project using the --namespace option to any command that operates on a project:

```
$ oc get templates --namespace openshift
```

The openshift project is a special project that acts as a repository for images and templates available for use by everyone in the OpenShift cluster. Although it doesn't appear in your own project list, you can still query it for certain information.

Adding a Collaborator

As the owner of a project, initially you are the only one who can access it and work in it. If you need to collaborate on a project with other users, you can add additional members to the project. When adding a user to the project, they can be added in one of three primary roles:

admin
> A project manager. The user will have rights to view any resource in the project and modify any resource in the project except for quotas. A user with this role for a project will be able to delete the project.

edit
> A user that can modify most objects in a project, but does not have the power to view or modify roles or bindings. A user with this role can create and delete applications in the project.

view
> A user who cannot make any modifications, but can see most objects in a project.

To add another user with edit role to the project, so they can create and delete applications, you need to use the oc adm policy command. You must be in the project when you run this command:

```
$ oc adm policy add-role-to-user edit <collaborator>
```

Replace *<collaborator>* with the name of the user as displayed by the oc whoami command when run by that user.

To remove a user from a project, run:

```
$ oc adm policy remove-role-from-user edit <collaborator>
```

To get a list of the users who have access to a project and their roles, a project manager can run the oc get rolebindings command.

Membership of a project can also be edited from the web console by going to the project list, clicking the three-dot menu icon for the project, and selecting View Membership.

Deploying Applications

Applications can be deployed to OpenShift in a number of different ways, using the web console and the command-line oc client.

The main methods for deploying an application are:

- From an existing container image hosted on an image registry located outside the OpenShift cluster.
- From an existing container image that has been imported into the image registry running inside the OpenShift cluster.
- From application source code in a Git repository hosting service. The application source code would be built into an image inside OpenShift, using an S2I builder.

- From image source code in a Git repository hosting service. The image source code would be built into an image inside OpenShift using instructions provided in a Dockerfile.

- From application source code pushed into OpenShift from a local filesystem using the command-line oc client. The application source code would be built into an image inside OpenShift using an S2I builder.

- From image source code pushed into OpenShift from a local filesystem using the command-line oc client. The image source code would be built into an image inside OpenShift using instructions provided in a Dockerfile.

To simplify deployment of applications that have multiple component parts, or that require configuration to be provided when creating the application, OpenShift provides a mechanism for defining *templates*. A template can be used to set up deployment of one or more applications at the same time using any of the methods listed. Parameters can be provided to a template when creating the applications, with values being used to fill out any configuration in resource objects that are defined by the template.

For maximum configurability and control, an application deployment can also be directly described using a list of the resource objects to be created. These lists can be provided as YAML or JSON.

Deploying from the Catalog

When you are in an empty project in the web console, you will be presented with the option, as shown in Figure 4-4, to add a new application to the project.

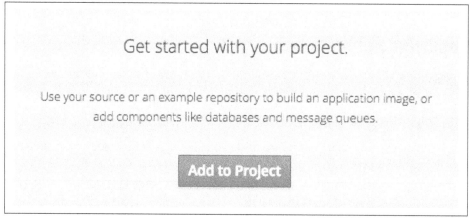

Figure 4-4. Addin an application to a project

Clicking on "Add to Project" will bring you to a catalog of application templates and S2I builders, as shown in Figure 4-5, that have been preinstalled into the OpenShift cluster. You can also get to this page by clicking "Add to Project" in the top banner of any project and selecting Browse Catalog.

Figure 4-5. Browsing the catalog

The catalog is constructed automatically from a number of sources.

The list of S2I builders you can use is derived by looking for images in the current project and the openshift project that have been labeled as builder images.

The list of application templates is generated by querying the list of template definitions in the current project and the openshift project.

The openshift project acts as a global repository for builder images and templates. If an administrator wants to make available a builder image or application template to the whole OpenShift cluster, this is where they should add them.

Because what is included in the openshift project is controlled by the administrator of the OpenShift cluster, what you find listed in the catalog may differ between OpenShift clusters. What appears can also differ based on whether OpenShift Origin or the Red Hat OpenShift Container Platform product is used.

From the command line, the list of application templates can be obtained using the command oc get templates. This will not return anything for an empty project or when no templates have been added to the project. To list the templates available in the openshift project, supply the --namespace openshift option.

To get a list of the images available, use the command `oc get imagestreams`. The `--namespace openshift` option should again be supplied to list those in the `openshift` project.

When you run this command, not all images listed may correspond to a builder image. This is because an image is also constructed for the application image created by running an S2I builder.

A better way of seeing from the command line what application templates and builder images are available is to run the `oc new-app -L` command. This produces a result similar to what would be available from the Browse Catalog page, combining application templates and builder images for both the current project and the `openshift` project in the output.

To search within the available application templates and builder images, use the filter field in the catalog browser. From the command line, you can use the `oc new-app -S` command, supplying the keyword to search for.

When you have found an entry matching what you need, you can select it from the web console. This will then send you through a forms-based workflow to deploy the application. On the command line, you will use `oc new-app`.

Deploying an Image

To deploy an existing container image, switch to the Deploy Image tab shown in Figure 4-6.

Figure 4-6. Deploying an image

To use an image that resides in the OpenShift cluster, select Image Stream Tag and then select the project that the image is owned by, the image, and the tag. You will be able to see only projects that you are the owner of, other projects that you have been explicitly granted access to, and the `openshift` project.

To use an image that is hosted on an image registry outside the OpenShift cluster, select Image Name and enter the name of the image, including the hostname of the image registry if using an image registry other than Docker Hub.

If using the command line, images hosted on any image registry can be deployed using the `oc new-app` command.

Deploying a Set of Resources

To deploy an application from a list of resource object definitions, switch to the Import YAML/JSON tab shown in Figure 4-7.

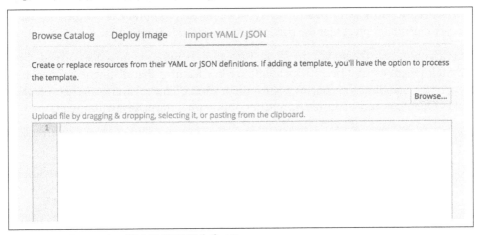

Figure 4-7. Importing YAML/JSON definitions

The YAML or JSON definition can be uploaded from your local computer or entered directly into the web page.

If you provide a template, you will be asked if you wish to apply the template immediately to deploy an application or load it, resulting in its then being selectable from the catalog browser and able to be used from the `oc` command-line client to deploy an application.

If using the command line, an application can be created from a set of resources or a template using `oc new-app` or `oc create`.

This book will not be going into details of how to create raw resource definitions or templates, or how to deploy an application using them. For further information see the OpenShift developer guide (*https://docs.openshift.org/latest/dev_guide/ index.html*).

Summary

Projects provide a space into which you can deploy your applications. You can choose to do everything within a single project, or use multiple projects and selectively enable access between projects so that different application components can communicate with each other.

The same features that provide isolation between your own projects are what are used to separate the projects of different users in a multitenant environment.

When you use OpenShift to deploy applications, you use your own user account, with controls on what you can do. As a developer, you would not use an admin account. If others need to work with you on an application, you can grant them the necessary access to just the project that the particular application is running in.

User accounts and the additional level of isolation between namespaces provided by the multitenant capabilities of OpenShift are key features that distinguish OpenShift from how a standard Kubernetes environment works. These features are part of what makes OpenShift more secure and a better option for enterprise environments.

## CHAPTER 5

Deploying Applications from Images

Now that you have created a project, you can move on to deploying an application.

In this chapter you will start out by deploying an application from a pre-existing container image hosted on an external image registry.

You would use this method if you created the image for the application outside the OpenShift cluster, or the image was being made available by a third party.

Once you have deployed the application, you will make it public so users can access it. You will then reconfigure the running application using environment variables, and scale up the number of instances of the application in order to handle a growing amount of traffic. You will also be shown how you can delete an application.

Deploying Your First Image

OpenShift supports deployment of container images hosted on any image registry that can be accessed from the OpenShift cluster. The first image you will deploy is stored on Docker Hub and is named *openshiftkatacoda/blog-django-py*. The application in the image implements a simple blog site.

The full name of the image used is *docker.io/openshiftkatacoda/blog-django-py*. When you leave off the hostname for the image registry, OpenShift will default to first looking for the image on any global image registries that a cluster admin has specified in the cluster configuration. It is typical to have the Docker Hub image registry included in that list. A company image registry or the Red Hat Container Registry might also be included.

To deploy the container image use the oc new-app command, providing it with the location of the image. The --name option is to set the name for the deployed application. If a name is not supplied, it will default to the last part of the image name. We'll use the name blog:

```
$ oc new-app openshiftkatacoda/blog-django-py --name blog
--> Found Docker image 0f405dd (5 days old) from Docker Hub
    for "openshiftkatacoda/blog-django-py"

    ...

      * An image stream will be created as "blog:latest" that will track
        this image
      * This image will be deployed in deployment config "blog"
      * Port 8080/tcp will be load balanced by service "blog"
        * Other containers can access this service through the hostname "blog"

--> Creating resources ...
    imagestream "blog" created
    deploymentconfig "blog" created
    service "blog" created
--> Success
    Run 'oc status' to view your app.
```

When you create the deployment, a series of resource objects will be created that tell OpenShift what it needs to do. In this case, an imagestream, deploymentconfig, and service were created.

The imagestream is a record of the image you want deployed. The deploymentconfig captures the details of how the deployment should be done. The service maintains a mapping to instances of your application so it can be accessed.

> Some resource object types have aliases that can be used in commands, or when they appear in command output. For example, svc can be used in place of service, dc in place of deploymentconfig, and is in place of imagestream. You can see a list of all resource object types and any name aliases by running oc get. You can see descriptions of the main resource object types by running oc types.

When a container image is deployed from the command line using oc new-app, the running container will not be visible outside the OpenShift cluster. In the case of a web application, you can make it visible by exposing the service. This is done using the oc expose command:

```
$ oc expose service/blog
route "blog" exposed
```

This will create a resource object called a route.

With the application deployed and visible, you can check on the status of the overall project using the oc status command:

```
$ oc status
In project My Project (myproject) on server https://127.0.0.1:8443

http://blog-myproject.127.0.0.1.nip.io to pod port 8080-tcp (svc/blog)
  dc/blog deploys istag/blog:latest
    deployment #1 deployed 1 minute ago - 1 pod

View details with 'oc describe <resource>/<name>' or list everything
with 'oc get all'.
```

To get a list of the instances of the application that were deployed you can use the command oc get pods:

```
$ oc get pods
NAME            READY   STATUS    RESTARTS   AGE
blog-1-36f46    1/1     Running   0          1m
```

There will be only one at this point.

To get a list of the resource objects created for the application you can use the oc get all command:

```
$ oc get all -o name --selector app=blog
imagestreams/blog
deploymentconfigs/blog
replicationcontrollers/blog-1
routes/blog
services/blog
pods/blog-1-36f46
```

To ensure only resources for the application you deployed are shown, you should use a selector and match on the label app=blog, which was added to all the resource objects created by the oc new-app and oc expose commands.

The pod resource object represents a group of one or more containers, although in most situations a pod would hold only one container. You will see a unique pod for each instance of your application. Containers in a pod are deployed together and are started, stopped, and replicated as a group.

A replicationcontroller is created from the deploymentconfig. It records a count of how many instances of your application should be running at any point in time. OpenShift will create as many pods as are needed to match the required count.

The OpenShift web console, shown in Figure 5-1, can also be used to view the application. You will find a summary for the deployed application in the project overview.

Figure 5-1. Blog site overview with route

Visit the URL displayed in the application summary with a web browser and you will be presented with the home page for the blog site (Figure 5-2).

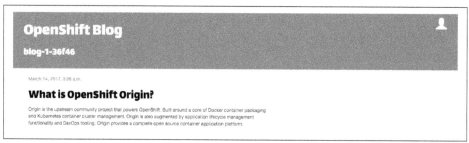

Figure 5-2. Blog site home page

You can also run the command oc get routes to see details of any services that have been exposed. The command will display the hostname that OpenShift has assigned to the application.

Scaling Up the Application

When oc new-app is used to deploy an application from a container image, only one instance of the application will be started. If you need to run more than once instance in order to handle the expected traffic, you can scale up the number of instances by running the oc scale command against the deployment configuration:

```
$ oc scale --replicas=3 dc/blog
deploymentconfig "blog" scaled
```

When the web application is scaled up, OpenShift will automatically reconfigure the router through which it is exposed to the public to load-balance between all instances of the application.

If you run oc get pods again, you should now see three instances of the application.

Instead of manually scaling the number of instances, you can enable automatic scaling based on metrics collected for an application. For further information, check out the OpenShift documentation on pod autoscaling (*https://docs.openshift.org/latest/dev_guide/pod_autoscaling.html*).

Runtime Configuration

Configuration for an application can be supplied by setting environment variables in the container or by mounting configuration files into the container.

You set required environment variables by using the --env option when running the oc new-app command:

```
$ oc new-app openshiftkatacoda/blog-django-py --name blog \
  --env BLOG_BANNER_COLOR=green
```

Optional environment variables can be set later by running the oc set env command against the deployment configuration:

```
$ oc set env dc/blog BLOG_BANNER_COLOR=green
deploymentconfig "blog" updated
```

When the environment variables are updated using oc set env, the application will be redeployed automatically with the new configuration. If you want to see what environment variables will be set in the container, you can use oc set env with the --list option:

```
$ oc set env dc/blog --list
# deploymentconfigs blog, container blog
BLOG_BANNER_COLOR=green
```

The topic of configuration and environment variables will be covered in more detail in Chapter 12.

Deleting the Application

When you no longer need the application, you can delete it using the `oc delete` command.

When doing this, you need to be selective about which resource objects you delete to ensure you delete only those for that particular application. This can be achieved by using the label that was applied by the `oc new-app` and `oc expose` commands to the resource objects created:

```
$ oc delete all --selector app=blog
imagestream "blog" deleted
deploymentconfig "blog" deleted
route "blog" deleted
service "blog" deleted
```

The `pod` and `replicationcontroller` may not be listed in the output from running `oc delete`, but they will be deleted. This is because they are deleted as a side effect of deleting the `deploymentconfig` for the application.

Deploying Using the Web Console

To deploy a pre-existing container image using the web console, select Add to Project from within a project and follow the steps outlined in Figure 5-3.

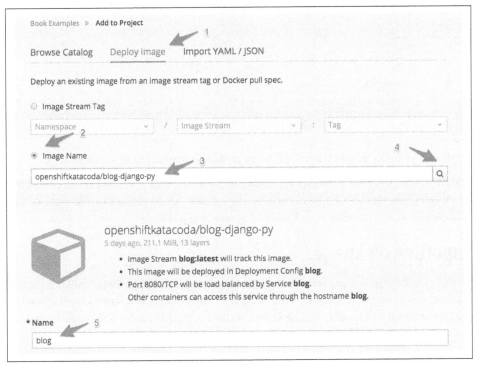

Figure 5-3. Deploy application image

❶ Click on the Deploy Image tab.

❷ Select Image Name to use an image stored on an external image registry.

❸ Enter **openshiftkatacoda/blog-django-py** as the value for Image Name.

❹ Press Enter, or click on the query icon to pull down details of the image.

❺ Change the name for the application to **blog**. The deployment for the image can be created by clicking Create at the bottom of the page.

The route to expose the service outside the OpenShift cluster can be created from the overview page for the project by selecting Create Route (Figure 5-4).

Networking

SERVICE Internal Traffic

blog

8080/TCP (8080-tcp) ⟶ 8080

ROUTES External Traffic

Create Route

Figure 5-4. The Create Route link

Services, networking, and routes will be covered in more detail in Chapter 13.

The overview page also provides the ability to scale up or down the number of instances of the deployed web application. Use the up and down arrows to the right of the circle showing the number and status of the running pods.

Importing an Image

When you deploy an application from an existing container image hosted on an external image registry, a copy of the image is downloaded and stored into an image registry internal to OpenShift. The image is then copied from there to each node in a cluster where the application is run.

In order to track the image that has been downloaded, an image stream definition is created. To see the list of the image stream definitions, run `oc get is`:

```
$ oc get is
NAME      DOCKER REPO                     TAGS      UPDATED
blog      172.30.118.67:5000/book/blog    latest    About a minute ago
```

The *<IP>:<PORT>* shown under DOCKER REPO is the address of the internal image registry.

Because the image is being used as part of an application deployment, it is labeled with the app label for the application. If you delete the application using the label, this will also delete the image stream and image.

If you need to deploy multiple separate applications from one image, you should import the image into OpenShift first using `oc import-image`:

```
$ oc import-image openshiftkatacoda/blog-django-py --confirm
The import completed successfully.

Name:               blog-django-py
...
```

You can then deploy the applications from the imported image:

```
$ oc new-app blog-django-py --name blog
```

In the web console, instead of the Image Name option on the Deploy Image page, you would use the Image Stream Tag option.

Because the image is imported prior to deploying an application, it is not tagged with the app label of a specific deployment. When you delete any of the applications using the label, you will not delete the image stream, leaving it in place for the other applications that depend on it.

Pushing to the Registry

The methods described thus far for deploying from an image relied on being able to pull the image from an external image registry. If you are using tools on your own local computer to build an image you can bypass the need to first push the image to an external image registry and instead push directly to the internal image registry of OpenShift.

To use the internal image registry, you need to know the address for accessing it. This information is not available from either the OpenShift web console or the oc command-line client, so you will need to ask the administrator for the OpenShift cluster if the internal image registry is accessible and what hostname and port it uses. If using a hosted OpenShift service, check its documentation.

For OpenShift Online, the internal image registry is accessible using an address of the form:

```
registry.<cluster-name>.openshift.com:443
```

To log in with the docker command, run:

```
$ docker login -u `oc whoami` -p `oc whoami --show-token` \
    registry.pro-us-east-1.openshift.com:443
Login Succeeded
```

Before you can push an image, you need to create an empty image stream for it using oc create imagestream.

```
$ oc create imagestream blog-django-py
```

Next, tag the local image you wish to push with the details of the image registry, your project in OpenShift, and the name of the image stream and image version tag:

```
$ docker tag blog-django-py \
    registry.pro-us-east-1.openshift.com:443/book/blog-django-py:latest
```

You are then ready to push the image to the OpenShift internal image registry:

```
$ docker push registry.pro-us-east-1.openshift.com:443/book/blog-django-py
```

The application can then be deployed using the image stream name.

Images and Security

When your application is deployed to OpenShift the default security model will enforce that it is run using an assigned Unix user ID unique to the project you are deploying it into. This behavior is implemented as part of the multitenant capabilities of OpenShift, but is also done to prevent images being run as the Unix *root* user.

Although containers provide a sandbox environment designed to prevent applications from being able to interact with the underlying host operating system, if a security vulnerability in the container runtime arose that allowed an application to break out of the sandbox, and the application were running as *root*, it could become *root* on the underlying host.

Best practice for images is to design them to be able to run as any Unix user ID. Many images available on public image registries do not adhere to such a practice and need to run as *root* to work, even though they have no requirement for elevated privileges.

This means that in a typical OpenShift environment, not all images you find on public image registries will work.

If it is your own image, you should redesign the image so it does not have to be run as *root*. If it does genuinely have a requirement to run as *root*, then only a cluster admin can grant the ability to do that.

To allow any applications deployed within a project the ability to run as the user the container image specifies, including *root*, a cluster admin can run against a project the command:

```
$ oadm policy add-scc-to-user anyuid -z default
```

A cluster admin would only want to allow this after the risks associated with running the image as *root* have been assessed. It is never good practice to run as *root* arbitrary images taken from public image registries.

For further information on this topic, see the OpenShift documentation on managing security context constraints (*https://docs.openshift.org/latest/admin_guide/ manage_scc.html*) and guidelines on creating images (*https://docs.openshift.org/latest/ creating_images/guidelines.html*).

Summary

Deploying a pre-existing container image in OpenShift is possible due to the Container as a Service (CaaS) capabilities provided by Kubernetes. When using a standard Kubernetes installation, the image would need to be pulled from an external image registry.

When using OpenShift, you can still pull images directly from an external image registry when deploying an application, but OpenShift also provides an image registry as part of the environment. You can push an image into the internal image registry, or you can set up an image stream definition such that, when deploying the image, it will be automatically pulled into and cached in the internal image registry. When deploying an image from the web console or command line, OpenShift will automatically set up this image stream for you.

Hosting of an image registry internal to OpenShift in order to cache images speeds up the ability to deploy applications. As when deploying an application to a node in a cluster, the image need only be pulled from the local internal image registry rather than having to reach out to the external image registry.

Although many images from external sources will work in OpenShift, the default restrictions in place, which prevent applications running as the Unix *root* user, may mean that images need to be modified to work. Alternatively, security can be relaxed to allow images to run as the user the image specifies. Best practice is to ensure images can run as an arbitrarily assigned Unix user ID and not as a specific Unix user ID.

## CHAPTER 6

Building and Deploying from Source

When you deploy a pre-existing container image, if this is your own image, it means you needed to have separate tooling available to construct that image. You also had to upload the image to an image registry from which OpenShift could pull it down, or push the image into the internal image registry of OpenShift.

To simplify the release management process for an application, OpenShift provides the ability to build the image for you. You would use this when you want to automate the complete workflow, including the building of the image, any testing of the image, and then deployment.

OpenShift provides four different build strategies:

Source
> This uses Source-to-Image to produce ready-to-run images by injecting application source (or other assets) into a builder image.

Docker
> This uses `docker build` to take a `Dockerfile` and associated source files and create a runnable image.

Pipeline
> This uses Jenkins and a workflow defined by a *Jenkinsfile* to create a pipeline for building a runnable image.

Custom
> This uses your own custom image to control the build process for creating the runnable image.

In this chapter you will learn how to use the Source build strategy to build and deploy an application from source code in a hosted Git repository, or source code pushed into OpenShift from your local computer.

Details of how to use the Docker build strategy will be covered in Chapter 7. However, this book will not go into the last two build strategies. See the OpenShift documentation for more details on the Pipeline (*http://bit.ly/2CynweL*) and Custom (*http://bit.ly/2CxoN5Y*) build strategies.

The Source Build Strategy

The Source build strategy uses the Source-to-Image (S2I) (*https://github.com/open shift/source-to-image*) tool to build a runnable image from your application source code. To build from application source, a hosted Git repository is required containing the source files. This Git repository must be accessible to the OpenShift cluster where you perform the builds.

OpenShift provides S2I builders for common programming languages including Java, NodeJS, Perl, PHP, Python, and Ruby. The builders will take your application source code, compile it if necessary, and integrate it with the application server stack provided with the builder image. When the container is run, the server will be started and your application code run.

Builder images are not restricted to being used to build applications from source code. Any form of input data can be combined with the builder image to create a runnable image.

To illustrate the Source build strategy, you will deploy the same web application as in the previous chapter. Whereas in the last chapter you deployed it using a pre-existing container image, this time you will deploy it from the application source code. The web application in question is implemented using the Python programming language, so you will use a Python S2I builder.

Deploying from Source

In the previous chapter, to deploy the blog site container image you used the command:

```
$ oc new-app openshiftkatacoda/blog-django-py --name blog
```

This took the pre-existing container image *openshiftkatacoda/blog-django-py* from Docker Hub, deployed it, and started up the web application.

To deploy from the application source code, this time use the command:

```
$ oc new-app --name blog \
    python:3.5~https://github.com/openshift-katacoda/blog-django-py
```

In place of the image name, the name of the S2I builder and a URL for a repository containing the source files for the web application are used. These are combined into a single argument to the command by inserting ~ between the two values. The oc `new-app` command will interpret this special combination as indicating that the Source build strategy should be used.

The result of running this command is:

```
--> Found image 956e2bd (5 days old) in image stream "openshift/python"
    under tag "3.5" for "python"

    Python 3.5
    ----------
    Platform for building and running Python 3.5 applications

    Tags: builder, python, python35, rh-python35

    * A source build using source code from
      https://github.com/openshift-katacoda/blog-django-py will be created
      * The resulting image will be pushed to image stream "blog:latest"
      * Use 'start-build' to trigger a new build
    * This image will be deployed in deployment config "blog"
    * Port 8080/tcp will be load balanced by service "blog"
      * Other containers can access this service through the hostname "blog"

--> Creating resources ...
    imagestream "blog" created
    buildconfig "blog" created
    deploymentconfig "blog" created
    service "blog" created
--> Success
    Build scheduled, use 'oc logs -f bc/blog' to track its progress.
    Run 'oc status' to view your app.
```

In addition to the resource objects created when you deployed from an image, a `buildconfig` has been created. This captures details on how to build the image inside OpenShift. A `buildconfig` can also be referenced using the bc alias.

To monitor the building of the application image as it occurs, you can run the command:

```
$ oc logs -f bc/blog
```

You can expose the service outside the OpenShift cluster by running:

```
$ oc expose svc/blog
```

Use the web console to view the URL for accessing the web application, or run the `oc get routes/blog` command to determine the unique hostname assigned to it. If you visit the site, you should again be presented with the blog site home page.

Creating a Separate Build

When the Source build strategy is invoked by oc new-app, it sets up two steps. The first step is to run the build using S2I, combining the source files with the builder image to create the runnable image. The second step is to deploy the runnable image and start up the web application.

You can perform the build step separately by running the oc new-build command instead of the oc new-app command:

```
$ oc new-build --name blog \
  python:3.5~https://github.com/openshift-katacoda/blog-django-py
  --> Found image 956e2bd (5 days old) in image stream "openshift/python"
      under tag "3.5" for "python"

      Python 3.5
      ----------
      Platform for building and running Python 3.5 applications

      Tags: builder, python, python35, rh-python35

      * A source build using source code from
        https://github.com/openshift-katacoda/blog-django-py will be created
        * The resulting image will be pushed to image stream "blog:latest"
        * Use 'start-build' to trigger a new build

  --> Creating resources with label build=blog ...
      imagestream "blog" created
      buildconfig "blog" created
  --> Success
      Build configuration "blog" created and build triggered.
      Run 'oc logs -f bc/blog' to stream the build progress.
```

The output looks similar, but the deploymentconfig and service resource objects are not created.

When the build has completed, the runnable image created is saved away as the image stream called blog. To deploy that image, the oc new-app command is used, but this time the name of the imagestream created by the build is supplied instead of the details of the builder image and repository URL:

```
$ oc new-app blog
  --> Found image 6792c9e (32 seconds old) in image stream "myproject/blog"
      under tag "latest" for "blog"

      myproject/blog-1:0b39e4f7
      -------------------------
      Platform for building and running Python 3.5 applications

      Tags: builder, python, python35, rh-python35
```

```
      * This image will be deployed in deployment config "blog"
      * Port 8080/tcp will be load balanced by service "blog"
        * Other containers can access this service through the hostname "blog"

  --> Creating resources ...
      deploymentconfig "blog" created
      service "blog" created
  --> Success
      Run 'oc status' to view your app.
```

The service once again can be exposed using oc expose.

Triggering a New Build

In the event that the source files used as input to the Source build strategy have changed, a new build can be triggered using the oc start-build command:

```
$ oc get bc
NAME      TYPE      FROM      LATEST
blog      Source    Git       1

$ oc start-build bc/blog
build "blog-2" started
```

Even though you created the build separately from setting up the deployment, when the build has completed and the imagestream updated, a redeployment will be automatically triggered. This occurs because oc new-app automatically sets up an image change trigger in the deployment configuration.

Triggers are also defined as part of the build configuration. The first of these is an additional image change trigger. This trigger will result in a rebuild if the S2I builder image python:3.5 is updated.

This is an important feature of the build process. When an S2I builder is used to create a number of different applications from different source files, if a security fix were available, pulling in an update to a builder image would automatically trigger a rebuild and redeployment of all the applications that use it. This makes it easy to quickly update applications when needing to patch images that they use.

When supplying the name of the S2I builder, if you do not specify a version tag, it will default to using the latest tag. In the case of the Python S2I builder, at the time of writing this book, latest mapped to 3.5. Were the S2I builder for Python 3.6 later installed and the latest tag remapped to reference it, this would result in the application being rebuilt with the newer version of Python. If your application code was not ready for Python 3.6, this could result in the build failing or your application not running correctly. It is recommended that where version tags are used on S2I builders you specify the exact version you want and avoid using latest.

Additional triggers are also defined in the build configuration to track source code changes. You can configure the hosting service for your source code repository to notify OpenShift whenever code changes are pushed to your repository. The source code trigger will then ensure the latest code is pulled down and the S2I build process run against it to generate the updated application image, with the application also being redeployed as a result. The topic of automating builds when source code changes are made will be covered further in Chapter 11.

Building from a Local Source

The build configuration that was set up used source files held in a hosted source code repository. To rebuild your application, your code changes had to be pushed up to the repository. Although the build is linked to the hosted source code repository, one-off builds can bypass the repository and use source files from a local filesystem.

Building from a local source is triggered using oc start-build, with the location of the local source directory specified using the --from-dir option:

```
$ oc start-build bc/blog --from-dir=.
Uploading directory "." as binary input for the build ...
build "blog-3" started
```

To revert to using source files held in the hosted code repository, start a new build without specifying an input source for the files:

```
$ oc start-build bc/blog
build "blog-4" started
```

Binary Input Builds

The variation on a build used to run a single build from a local source is called a *binary input* source build. This is useful during the development of an application, as you can iterate on changes without needing to commit and push changes up to the repository. You only commit and push up changes when you have checked the result and are finished.

A build configuration can be set up from the outset as a binary input source build. In this configuration it would not be linked to a hosted source code repository, and all builds would need to be triggered manually and the source files supplied.

To create a binary input build configuration, use `oc new-build` and supply the `--binary` option:

```
$ oc new-build --name blog --binary --strategy=source --image-stream python:3.5
--> Found image 440f01a (6 days old) in image stream "openshift/python"
    under tag "3.5" for "python"

    Python 3.5
    ----------
    Platform for building and running Python 3.5 applications

    Tags: builder, python, python35, rh-python35

    * A source build using binary input will be created
      * The resulting image will be pushed to image stream "blog:latest"
      * A binary build was created, use 'start-build --from-dir' to trigger
        a new build

--> Creating resources with label build=blog ...
    imagestream "blog" created
    buildconfig "blog" created
--> Success
```

The initial and subsequent builds are triggered using `oc start-build`, supplying the `--from-dir` option to use source files from a local directory:

```
$ oc start-build blog --from-dir=.
Uploading directory "." as binary input for the build ...
build "blog-1" started
```

Because the build configuration isn't linked to a source code repository and `oc start-build` must be manually run each time, applications cannot be automatically rebuilt and redeployed if an S2I builder image has changed. This is because the input source would not be available to the build.

Binary input builds are useful where you have an existing toolchain for creating application binaries or components to be included in an image. An example is creating a Java WAR file and then using an S2I builder to inject that into a base image containing the Java servlet container runtime.

Testing the Container Image

The image created by the build process, when deployed, will be untested. If you want to be able to run unit tests on the application source code used in the build or verify the image before it's pushed to the internal image registry, you can use a post-commit hook on a build.

The test is run by launching a new container with the recently built image and running the post-commit hook command inside the container. If the command run by the build hook returns a nonzero exit code, the resulting image will not be pushed to the registry and the build will be marked as having failed.

To specify the command to run as the post-commit hook, run the `oc set build-hook` command. For example:

```
$ oc set build-hook bc/blog --post-commit --script "powershift image verify"
```

When the `--script` option is used to specify the command, the original image entrypoint will be left as is, with the image command being overridden. If the `--command` option is used to specify the command, it will be used to replace the original image entrypoint. If `--` is used, arguments to pass to the original image command can be supplied.

To remove a build hook, the `--remove` option can be used.

When running unit tests from a post-commit hook, you should avoid contacting other services, as the container will be run in the same project as your deployed application. This is to avoid accidentally running tests against your production services. If a database is required for the tests, run a local filesystem–based database such as SQLite.

For more complex end-to-end integration tests, use a separate project from your production environment for running builds and tests. When the image has passed tests, you can promote it into the project used for production. Pipelines using an integrated Jenkins installation can be used to manage advanced builds. For more details see the OpenShift documentation on pipelines (*https://docs.openshift.org/latest/dev_guide/openshift_pipeline.html*).

Build and Runtime Configuration

Similarly to when deploying an application from a container image, environment variables to be set when the container is run can be specified using the `--env` option to `oc new-app`. This can be done when deploying directly from source code, or when using `oc new-app` to deploy the image created by a distinct build step.

If it is necessary to set environment variables for the build step and you are deploying directly from source code, use the `--build-env` option to `oc new-app`:

```
$ oc new-app --name blog --build-env UPGRADE_PIP_TO_LATEST=1 \
    python:3.5~https://github.com/openshift-katacoda/blog-django-py
```

If using the two-step approach of invoking `oc new-build` and `oc new-app`, the environment variables specific to the build step should be passed to `oc new-build` using the `--env` option:

```
$ oc new-build --name blog --env UPGRADE_PIP_TO_LATEST=1 \
    python:3.5~https://github.com/openshift-katacoda/blog-django-py
```

If the environment variables need to be added after the build configuration has been created, the `oc set env` command can be used:

```
$ oc set env bc/blog UPGRADE_PIP_TO_LATEST=1
buildconfig "blog" updated
```

Build-time environment variables might be required to set proxy details or customize the build process implemented by the S2I builder. You can see the environment variables that are being set for the build by using `oc set env` with the `--list` option.

```
$ oc set env bc/blog --list
# buildconfigs blog
UPGRADE_PIP_TO_LATEST=1
```

Although the environment variables are specified in the build configuration, they will also be set in the image created and visible to the application when it is deployed.

Summary

The ability to deploy an application from source code, with OpenShift building the application image for you, is a feature of the Platform as a Service (PaaS) capabilities provided by OpenShift. This is an additional layer of functionality that is built on top of Kubernetes.

The Source build strategy uses the Source-to-Image tool to build a runnable image from your application source code. OpenShift provides S2I builders for many common programming languages. You can also create your own S2I builder images if you need to support a custom application stack.

An automated build and deployment mechanism means that when the build is complete and any tests successfully run, the application image will be deployed.

## CHAPTER 7

Building an Image from a Dockerfile

Using an S2I builder to create an application image simplifies the build process, as the builder does all the hard work for you. To make it simple, the author of the S2I builder will have made some decisions in advance about what application server stack is used, how it is configured, and how your application source code needs to be structured.

Although you can override the S2I build and deployment process for an application, the extent of the customizations you can make is restricted. You cannot, for example, install additional operating system packages or run any actions that require root privileges.

In order to have full control over how the image is built and the application run, you will need to use the Docker build strategy.

In this chapter you will learn how you can build a container image in OpenShift from a Dockerfile using the Docker build strategy. The container image produced can be an application image or your own custom S2I builder image.

The Docker Build Strategy

The Docker build strategy takes the instructions from a Dockerfile and uses them to construct a container image. The Dockerfile and associated files required to construct the image need to be in a hosted source code repository accessible to the OpenShift cluster where you perform the builds.

This strategy can be used to construct an application image or an S2I builder image. By having OpenShift perform the build, you avoid the need to have separate infrastructure to create the image. The building of the image can also be linked via image triggers to any builds or deployments dependent on the image. An update to the image will therefore trigger the subsequent builds and deployments, automating your workflow.

To illustrate how to set up a build from a *Dockerfile*, we are going to build the same image we used in Chapter 5 to deploy our blog site, but do it inside OpenShift. We will then do a quick recap on how to deploy the image. This time we will use the locally built image rather than that we pulled down from the external image registry.

Security and Docker Builds

Before using this build strategy it is important to be aware of the security implications of using it.

The build strategy works by using the `docker build` command to process the instructions contained in the `Dockerfile`. Although the build process is initiated from a container, it is necessary for it to run as the *root* user. This is so that it has the appropriate privileges to interact with the Docker daemon. The build of the image by the Docker daemon also runs as *root* in order to perform actions such as installing the system packages required by the image.

Because of the risks that exist when running as *root*, even inside a container, the ability to run any container as *root* may be disabled in an OpenShift cluster. As a consequence, the ability to use this build strategy may not be present in the OpenShift cluster you are using.

Creating the Build

For this build you will use the same source code repository as was used for the Source build strategy, but direct `oc new-app` to run the build with the Docker build strategy. This is done by passing the `--strategy=docker` option, along with the URL for the repository:

```
$ oc new-build --name blog --strategy=docker \
  https://github.com/openshift-katacoda/blog-django-py
  --> Found Docker image 956e2bd (5 days old) from Docker Hub
      for "centos/python-35-centos7:latest"

      ...

        * An image stream will be created as "python-35-centos7:latest"
          that will track the source image
        * A Docker build using source code from
          https://github.com/openshift-katacoda/blog-django-py will be
          created
          * The resulting image will be pushed to image stream "blog:latest"
          * Every time "python-35-centos7:latest" changes a new build will
            be triggered
```

```
--> Creating resources with label build=blog ...
    imagestream "python-35-centos7" created
    imagestream "blog" created
    buildconfig "blog" created
--> Success
    Build configuration "blog" created and build triggered.
    Run 'oc logs -f bc/blog' to stream the build progress.
```

The build, when run, will use the Dockerfile in the repository as the source of instructions for how to build the image.

Deploying the Image

With the build complete, the resulting image is stored in your project as the image stream called blog. To deploy the image as an application use the oc new-app command:

```
$ oc new-app blog
--> Found image 1f6debb (5 minutes old) in image stream "myproject/blog"
    under tag "latest" for "blog"

    ...

    * This image will be deployed in deployment config "blog"
    * Port 8080/tcp will be load balanced by service "blog"
      * Other containers can access this service through the
        hostname "blog"

--> Creating resources ...
    deploymentconfig "blog" created
    service "blog" created
--> Success
    Run 'oc status' to view your app.
```

In this case, because you went on to deploy the image as an application, you could instead have used the oc new-app command and gone directly from source files to the deployed application:

```
$ oc new-app --name blog --strategy=docker \
  https://github.com/openshift-katacoda/blog-django-py
```

You would use oc new-build rather than oc new-app when creating an S2I builder image from a Dockerfile. In that case the final image wouldn't be able to be deployed as an application.

Build and Runtime Configuration

Similarly to when deploying an application from a container image, environment variables to be set when the container is run can be specified using the --env option to oc new-app. This can be done when deploying directly from source code, or when using oc new-app to deploy the image created by a distinct build step.

If it is necessary to set environment variables for the build step and you are deploying directly from source code, use the --build-env option to oc new-app:

```
$ oc new-app --name blog --strategy=docker \
  --build-env UPGRADE_PIP_TO_LATEST=1 \
  https://github.com/openshift-katacoda/blog-django-py
```

If using the two-step approach of invoking oc new-build and oc new-app, the environment variables specific to the build step should be passed to oc new-build using the --env option:

```
$ oc new-build --name blog --strategy=docker \
  --env UPGRADE_PIP_TO_LATEST=1 \
  https://github.com/openshift-katacoda/blog-django-py
```

If the environment variables need to be added after the build configuration has been created, the oc set env command can be used:

```
$ oc set env bc/blog UPGRADE_PIP_TO_LATEST=1
buildconfig "blog" updated
```

Build-time environment variables might be required to customize the build process when the image is being built. You can see the environment variables that are being set for the build by using oc set env with the --list option:

```
$ oc set env bc/blog --list
# buildconfigs blog
UPGRADE_PIP_TO_LATEST=1
```

Although the environment variables are specified in the build configuration, they will also be set in the image created and visible to the application when it is deployed.

When building an image from a Dockerfile, it is also possible to supply build arguments. These behave like environment variables, except that they will not be set in the container when the image is run, only during the build.

A build argument can be set using the --build-arg option when using oc new-build:

```
$ oc new-build --name blog --strategy=docker \
  --build-arg HTTP_PROXY=https://proxy.example.com \
  https://github.com/openshift-katacoda/blog-django-py
```

To use build arguments, an appropriate ARG instruction must have been defined in the Dockerfile; otherwise, they will be ignored.

Although an environment variable corresponding to the build argument will not be set in the container when the image is run, if you are able to access the image directly from the image registry, you will be able to see the value associated with a build argument using docker history or docker inspect.

Using an Inline Dockerfile

Images can be customized by creating a new image that derives from an existing image. Additional layers are then added, which include further software packages or configuration. This can be done using the Docker build strategy, with the Dockerfile and associated files being hosted in a source code repository. A binary input build could also be used, enabling the files to be held in a local filesystem and injected into the build process.

For simple image customizations where all the steps can be described in the Docker file, with no additional files needing to be supplied along with the Dockerfile, the Dockerfile can be defined as part of the build configuration. This approach could be used when you need to install additional operating system packages or utilities required by an application built using an S2I builder.

To illustrate this case, create a Dockerfile with the additional steps:

```
FROM openshift/python:3.5
USER root
RUN yum install -y wget
USER 1001
```

You can then use a Docker build to create a new image using the *Dockerfile* as input by running oc new-build with the --dockerfile option:

```
$ cat Dockerfile | oc new-build --name python-plus --dockerfile=-
--> Found image a080357 (2 days old) in image stream "openshift/python" under
    tag "3.5" for "openshift/python:3.5"

    ...

    * A Docker build using a predefined Dockerfile will be created
      * The resulting image will be pushed to image stream "python-plus:latest"
      * Use 'start-build' to trigger a new build

--> Creating resources with label build=python-plus ...
    imagestream "python-plus" created
    buildconfig "python-plus" created
--> Success
    Build configuration "python-plus" created and build triggered.
    Run 'oc logs -f bc/python-plus' to stream the build progress.
```

The argument of - to the --dockerfile option says to read the Dockerfile contents from standard input over a pipe—otherwise, the contents of the Dockerfile would need to be supplied as the value for the option. It is not possible to provide a path specifying the location of the Dockerfile in the filesystem.

When the build has completed, the customized image can be used in place of the original S2I builder image by using the name of the imagestream created in place of the original builder name.

Summary

As an extension to the traditional PaaS functionality of being able to build from application source code with the platform worrying about the details, OpenShift also supports building a container image from instructions in a Dockerfile.

This provides the most flexibility for controlling how the container image is built and run, and offers the ability to install additional operating system packages into the container image.

Because this build strategy requires the build to run as the Unix *root* user, however, it may not be enabled for the OpenShift cluster you are using.

## CHAPTER 8

Understanding Source-to-Image Builders

The Docker build strategy provides the most control over how to build an image. Because of the potential security risks with allowing Docker builds within a shared OpenShift cluster, the ability to use the Docker build strategy would usually be restricted to trusted developers.

The most common method for building applications is therefore using the S2I builders. To get the most out of the S2I builders, it is helpful to understand how they work.

In this chapter you will delve into how S2I builders work and how to implement a simple S2I builder image. You will also be shown how to add annotations to the image for your custom S2I builder so that it can be selected and used from the OpenShift web console.

The Source-to-Image Project

The process of building an image from application source code in OpenShift makes use of a toolkit and workflow originating from the open source Source-to-Image (*https://github.com/openshift/source-to-image*) project.

The S2I toolkit produces ready-to-run images by injecting source files into a running instance of a builder base image, with scripts in the builder image turning that source code into a runnable application. From the container the build process was run in, a runnable application image is then created.

The command-line tool that drives the S2I build process is called s2i. When you deploy an application from source code in OpenShift using S2I, all the steps involved in running the s2i command-line tool are done for you. It is possible, however, to use this tool on your own system to create container images, independent of OpenShift.

To illustrate how the S2I build process works, we will use the `s2i` command-line tool directly.

Building the Application Image

To build an application image using the `s2i` command-line tool, you need two inputs. The first is your application source code. The second is an S2I builder image that supports the programming language and server stack your application is implemented in.

S2I builder images are normal container images, with many available on the Docker Hub image registry. Examples of images for commonly used programming languages or application server stacks are:

Node.js 6	centos/*nodejs-6-centos7*
Ruby 2.3	centos/*ruby-23-centos7*
Perl 5.24	centos/*perl-524-centos7*
PHP 7.0	centos/*php-70-centos7*
Python 3.5	centos/*python-35-centos7*
Wildfly 10.1	openshift/*wildfly-101-centos7*

Application source code can be hosted on a Git repository hosting service, or you can keep it in a local filesystem directory.

To create a runnable container image using the `s2i` command-line tool, you will also need to have a local container service running.

To build the container image, run `s2i build`, supplying it the location of your application source code, the name of the S2I builder image, and the name to give to the application image created:

```
$ s2i build https://github.com/openshift-katacoda/blog-django-py \
    centos/python-35-centos7 blog
```

Details of the image produced can be viewed by running `docker images`:

```
$ docker images
REPOSITORY   TAG      IMAGE ID       CREATED          SIZE
blog         latest   ec50f4d34a83   About a minute ago  675MB
```

Using `s2i`, you can create an application image without needing to know how to create a `Dockerfile`, and without needing to know how to run `docker build`.

To run the application image, use `docker run`:

```
$ docker run --rm -p 8080:8080 blog
```

Although the process of generating the application image may appear to be magic, the resulting image isn't special. You can build images outside OpenShift using `s2i` and run them using a local container service, share them with others by pushing them to an image registry, or deploy them to OpenShift.

Using the S2I support in OpenShift does have the benefits, though, of tying into the automated build and deployment mechanism. Chapter 11 will look more into automating builds and deployments using OpenShift.

Assembling the Source Code

When the `s2i build` command is run, a number of steps are performed to create the application image.

The first step is to package up the application source code into an archive.

In our case, the `s2i build` command was provided with a URL to application source code on a Git repository hosting service. The `s2i` command will download the latest version of the source code. An alternative version could have been nominated by supplying a tag name, commit reference, or branch name, and instead of a remote Git repository, a path to a local directory containing the application source code could have been provided.

The second step is that the `s2i` command will use the `docker run` command to start a container from the S2I builder image. At the same time, it will inject the archive containing the application source code into the container.

The command run in the container by the `s2i` command will unpack the archive containing the application source code. An *assemble* script provided by the S2I builder image will then be run.

It is this *assemble* script that takes the application source code and moves it into the correct location, or compiles the source code to produce a runnable application. As part of this build process, the *assemble* script might also download any language-specific packages that the application requires to run, and install them.

Once the *assemble* script has completed, the third and final step of converting the snapshot of the stopped container into a runnable image is performed. When this is done, the `s2i` command will also set the program to be executed when the image is run to be a *run* script provided by the S2I builder image.

It is this *run* script that is executed when the `docker run` command is used to run the image. The *run* script will perform any steps required to start up the application prepared by the *assemble* script.

Creating an S2I Builder Image

As an S2I builder is a container image, you can create your own custom builder images. This is done by building an image from a `Dockerfile`. The OpenShift project provides a convenient base image (*https://github.com/sclorg/s2i-base-container*) you can use as a starting point for a custom S2I builder.

To illustrate a simple S2I builder, you can create a builder for running a web server for hosting static files. The source files provided to the builder when the S2I process is run will be what the web server hosts and makes available.

The `Dockerfile` for this builder would contain:

```
FROM openshift/base-centos7

LABEL io.k8s.description="Simple HTTP Server" \
      io.k8s.display-name="Simple HTTP Server" \
      io.openshift.s2i.scripts-url="image:///usr/libexec/s2i" \
      io.openshift.expose-services="8080:http" \
      io.openshift.tags="builder,http"

COPY assemble /usr/libexec/s2i/
COPY run /usr/libexec/s2i/
COPY usage /usr/libexec/s2i/

EXPOSE 8080

USER 1001

CMD [ "/usr/libexec/s2i/usage" ]
```

The `Dockerfile` needs to define the `io.openshift.s2i.scripts-url` label as the location of the *assemble* and *run* scripts in the image, with the scripts being copied into that location.

The `io.openshift.expose-services` label, along with the `EXPOSE` statement, tells OpenShift which ports the application produced by the builder will use.

The `Dockerfile` can include any `RUN` statements required to install additional packages when the builder image is built.

The `USER` statement must be set at the end of the `Dockerfile` to the user ID `1001`, which will be the user the build process runs as.

The *usage* script included in the image is configured as the default command executed when the image is run. It has the following contents:

```
#!/bin/bash

cat <<EOF
This is a S2I builder image for running a simple HTTP server. For
```

```
instructions on using the S2I builder image see:

* https://github.com/openshift-katacoda/simple-http-server
EOF
```

The *usage* script is provided as a way for users to find information on how to use your builder image.

The main work in preparing the image is done by the *assemble* script, which looks like this:

```
#!/bin/bash

echo " -----> Move HTTP server files into place."

mv /tmp/src/* /opt/app-root/src/
```

The *assemble* script should take any source files placed in the */tmp/src* directory by the `s2i build` process and copy them into the required location, or compile them into an executable application.

The *assemble* script could also download and install additional language-specific packages required by the application, which are listed in a package dependencies file included with the source files.

For the `openshift/base-centos7` image used, the home directory when running the build and the application is set as */opt/app-root/src*. An application can write to any location under */opt/app-root*.

Although not required in this example, if the application, when run, needs to write to the filesystem, you need to ensure you fix up permissions on the directory tree at */opt/app-root* after any custom build steps have been run. The base builder image provides a *fix-permissions* script for this. When run, the *fix-permissions* script will ensure that all directories and files in the directory passed as an argument are writable by any user in the same group. If this step is required, you would add it to the end of the *assemble* script:

```
fix-permissions /opt/app-root
```

The *run* script is executed when the application image produced by the S2I build process is run. It looks like this:

```
#!/bin/bash

echo " -----> Run HTTP server."

exec python -m SimpleHTTPServer 8080
```

The application you run from this script should be run in the foreground, and the exec statement should be used when executing it. This ensures that it inherits process

ID 1 of the container, allowing the application to receive any signals sent to the container to trigger a shutdown.

With both the *assemble* and *run* scripts, if any step in the scripts fails, the script as a whole should fail immediately. The easiest way of ensuring this, without needing to check the result of every command run, is to add this line at the start of each script:

```
set -eo pipefail
```

This command instructs the *bash* interpreter to exit immediately when any command run returns a result indicating a failure.

Building the S2I Builder Image

If using the `s2i` command-line tool outside OpenShift, to build the S2I builder image from these files, you would run:

```
$ docker build -t simple-http-server .
```

This would produce an image called `simple-http-server`. To use this to build an application image, you would run:

```
$ s2i build \
  https://github.com/example/static-web-site \
  simple-http-server \
  static-web-site
```

The *run* script in this builder starts the simple HTTP server to host the files copied into the image. To run the application image, use this command:

```
$ docker run --rm -p 8080:8080 static-web-site
```

Using the S2I Builder with OpenShift

To use your S2I builder image in OpenShift, you have three options.

The first is to build it outside of OpenShift, as shown previously, and upload it to an external image registry such as Docker Hub. This example has been placed on Docker Hub as *openshiftkatacoda/simple-http-server*. You would import it into OpenShift using:

```
$ oc import-image openshiftkatacoda/simple-http-server --confirm
```

This will create an image stream called `simple-http-server`, and you can use it by running:

```
$ oc new-app simple-http-server~https://github.com/example/static-web-site
```

The second option is, rather than uploading the image to an external image registry, to push it to the internal image registry of OpenShift. How to do this was described in Chapter 5.

The final option is to build the S2I builder image in OpenShift. The source files for this example can be found on GitHub (*https://github.com/openshift-katacoda/simple-http-server*).

To build it in OpenShift you would run:

```
$ oc new-build --name simple-http-server --strategy=docker \
  --code https://github.com/openshift-katacoda/simple-http-server
```

```
$ oc start-build simple-http-server
```

This would again create an image stream called `simple-http-server`, which would be used as shown previously.

Adding an S2I Builder to the Catalog

In order to have your S2I builder be selectable in the catalog of the web console, an additional step of adding an annotation to the image stream definition for the S2I builder image is required. This can be done by editing the image stream using the command:

```
$ oc edit is/simple-http-server
```

The `tags` annotation with value `builder` should be added, yielding:

```
{
    "kind": "ImageStream",
    "apiVersion": "v1",
    "metadata": {
        "name": "simple-http-server"
    },
    "spec": {
        "tags": [
            {
                "name": "latest",
                "annotations": {
                    "tags": "builder"
                },
                "from": {
                    "kind": "DockerImage",
                    "name": "openshiftkatacoda/simple-http-server:latest"
                }
            }
        ]
    }
}
```

At the time of writing this book, the `tags` annotation has to be added for each image version tag. A proposal exists to allow it to be defined as an annotation within the metadata of the image stream, and by the time you read this book, that may be supported.

In the catalog of the web console, you can now search for `simple-http-server` and create your application using the builder from your browser.

Additional annotations can be added to the image stream definition to provide a display name, description, and category. For addition information, see the OpenShift documentation on writing image streams for S2I builders (*http://bit.ly/2EG4w47*).

If you want to make it simple for others to use your S2I builder, and the image is hosted on Docker Hub, you can host the image stream definition using any web server. A user can then load the image stream definition using `oc create`, in place of using `oc import-image`. For this example builder, you could instead run:

```
$ oc create -f https://raw.githubusercontent.com\
/openshift-katacoda/simple-http-server/master/imagestream.json
```

Summary

The Source-to-Image tool implements a mechanism to take application source code and build it into a container image. The tool works by starting a container using an S2I builder image, injecting the application source code into the container, and running an *assemble* script to set up the contents of the image.

The S2I tool is a standalone application you can use on your own local system, independent of any platform for deploying applications to containers. To make it easier to use, OpenShift provides integrated support for the tool, which forms the core of the PaaS functionality of OpenShift.

OpenShift provides a range of S2I builders you can use, or you can easily create your own custom S2I builders and integrate them into OpenShift so you can choose them from the OpenShift web console.

## CHAPTER 9

Customizing Source-to-Image Builds

Rather than creating an S2I builder from scratch, it is more typical that you will require only minor customizations to the behavior of the S2I builder image for a specific application.

A well-designed S2I builder image should provide the ability to customize the behavior for common use cases using environment variables set during the build or at the time of deployment.

When the S2I builder doesn't do this, or your use case requires additional steps to be run, you will need to override the behavior of the default *assemble* and *run* scripts.

In this chapter you will learn about the different ways that the S2I *assemble* and *run* scripts can be overridden or extended. This can be done by including different versions of the scripts with your application source code; by hosting them on a separate web server and referencing them from the build configuration; or, if you only wish to override the *run* script, by mounting it into a container from a config map or persistent volume.

You will also learn how you can create a modified S2I builder by using the Source build strategy to build the image, rather than the Docker build strategy.

Using Environment Variables

When using an existing S2I builder, the hope is that the authors of that builder have designed it with flexibility in mind—that is, that they have allowed the behavior of the S2I builder to be customized through configuration, both when the builder is being run to create an application image and when that application image is being run.

Configuration for a builder can be supplied using environment variables. You saw in Chapter 6 how environment variables can be set for the deployment of an application, or when the application is being built using an S2I builder.

In the prior examples, the environment variables were set as part of the build and deployment configuration within OpenShift. One problem with defining environment variables as part of the configuration in OpenShift is that it is separate to the source code for the application and not under version control.

Where it makes more sense to include these environment variables with the source code, when using an S2I builder, they can be added as part of the source code in the file *.s2i/environment*.

Instead of using the `--build-env` option to `oc new-app` or `oc new-build`, you would create the *.s2i/environment* file and place entries in it of the form `key=value`. For example:

```
UPGRADE_PIP_TO_LATEST=1
```

Only static values can be specified in this file. It is not possible to add values for environment variables that are dynamically calculated from other values or by running a command.

Environment variables set in this file will become part of the application image and will be present for the building of the application image as well as when it is deployed.

Overriding the Builder Scripts

When the S2I builder is run to build an application image, the *assemble* script contained in the image is run to take source files and generate the runnable application. When the application image is later run, the *run* script contained in the image is used to run the application.

Both the *assemble* and *run* scripts can be overridden by supplying your own scripts in the `.s2i/bin` directory of the application source code. If present, these will be copied into the container during the S2I build process, with the *assemble* script being run in place of the default script. Similarly, if a replacement *run* script is supplied, it will be used when the application image is run.

Although these scripts could be self-contained and completely replace the original scripts, the more typical use case is to perform some action and then execute the original script. In the case of the *assemble* script, you might also perform additional actions after the original *assemble* script is executed.

A custom *assemble* script added as *.s2i/bin/assemble* would therefore take the form:

```
#!/bin/bash
```

```
set -eo pipefail

# Set environment variables.

# ...

# Execute original assemble script.

/usr/libexec/s2i/assemble

# Run additional build steps.

# ...
```

Ensure the script is executable. Being a shell script, you can include any shell code in it, including code that dynamically sets environment variables.

Remember that it is the original *assemble* script that will copy source files into place, install additional packages, or compile the source files into an application executable. If you need to do more than set and export environment variables prior to the original *assemble* script being run, the source files copied in for the build will be in the */tmp/src* directory.

If you were overriding the *run* script by adding *.s2i/bin/run*, it would take the form:

```
#!/bin/bash

set -eo pipefail

# Set environment variables.

# ...

# Run additional deployment steps.

# ...

# Execute original run script.

exec /usr/libexec/s2i/run
```

When running the original *run* script, you must use exec. This ensures that the original script gets to run as process ID 1 in the container and is able to receive signals sent to the container to shut down the application.

Because the original *run* script replaces the execution of this script, you cannot run any post-deployment steps. If you need to run actions after the rollout of a new version of an application you should look at using lifecycle hooks. Lifecycle hooks will be covered in more detail in Chapter 17.

Read-Only Code Repositories

Adding *assemble* and *run* scripts to the application source files can only be done if you own the original source code, or if the application source code is using a hosted Git repository and you have forked the original code repository.

If you can't add to the original source files, or don't want to, you can instead host the *assemble* and *run* scripts in a separate code repository and set up the build configuration to download them from that location. To do this, you need to edit the build configuration and set the `spec.strategy.sourceStrategy.scripts` property to the URL of a directory on a web server from which the *assemble* and *run* scripts can be downloaded. This cannot be done at the time of creating an application using `oc new-app` or from the web console unless you are supplying the raw resource object definitions for the build and deployment.

To set this property for a build configuration that has already been created, you can use the web console or `oc edit`, and change the YAML/JSON definition of the build configuration directly.

You can also edit it from the command line by using `oc patch`:

```
$ oc patch bc/blog --type=json --patch \
  '[{"op":"add",
     "path":"/spec/strategy/sourceStrategy/scripts",
     "value":"https://raw.githubusercontent.com/example/test/master"}]'
```

If this method is used and the application source code also provided *assemble* and *run* scripts in the *.s2i/bin* directory, the files in the application source code will be ignored and will not be copied into the image. This means that the versions of the scripts specified from the build configuration using the URL cannot call the existing *assemble* and *run* scripts present in the application source code. These scripts can, however, still execute the original *assemble* and *run* scripts provided by the S2I builder image.

Overriding the Runtime Image

The methods described previously override the *assemble* and *run* scripts at the time that the application image is being built. If you have an existing image and need to override the *run* script, but do not want to rebuild the image, it is possible to override the command used when the container is started. This can be done by editing the deployment configuration for the application deployed from the image.

In this situation, the replacement *run* script will need to be stored in a persistent volume, provided using a config map item mounted as a file into the container, or placed in a temporary volume using an init container.

If using a config map, first create it:

```
$ oc create configmap blog-run-script --from-file=run
```

Next, mount the config map into the container:

```
$ oc set volume dc/blog --add --type=configmap \
  --configmap-name=blog-run-script \
  --mount-path=/opt/app-root/scripts
```

Then update the deployment configuration to execute this script when starting the container:

```
$ oc patch dc/blog --type=json --patch \
 '[{"op":"add",
     "path":"/spec/template/spec/containers/0/command",
     "value":["bash","/opt/app-root/scripts/run"]}]'
```

Because you are using a config map, the *run* script will not be marked as executable. It is therefore necessary to use *bash* to execute the *run* script.

If using a mounted persistent volume, copy the *run* script into the persistent volume using oc rsync, or create an interactive terminal session in the container using the web console or oc rsh and edit the *run* script in place. When storing the *run* script in a persistent volume you can mark it as executable and directly execute it as the command in the deployment configuration.

To use an init container, you would mount a volume of type emptyDir within the init container and place the *run* script in it. The main application container would mount the same volume and run the script from it. You can find additional information on using volumes in Chapter 14 and init containers in Chapter 17.

Updating the Image Metadata

In the cases described here where the *assemble* and *run* scripts were overridden by new versions that were either placed in the *.s2i/bin* directory of the application source code or supplied by specifying a web server from which to download the scripts, those new versions only affected the specific image being created. If you were to take the image created from the S2I build process and attempt to use it as an S2I builder image, the latter build would revert to using the original scripts provided in the first builder image.

In order to use an S2I build to create a new S2I builder image that behaves differently, it is necessary to override the metadata of the image created. This can be done from an *assemble* script by creating the file */tmp/.s2i/image_metadata.json* and overriding the labels for the image that specify where the *assemble* and *run* scripts are located.

Starting with the source files from the simple-http-server image created in Chapter 8 from a Dockerfile, add the file *.s2i/bin/assemble*, containing:

```
#!/bin/bash

set -eo pipefail

# Move assemble/run scripts to new location.

mkdir /opt/app-root/s2i

mv /tmp/src/* /opt/app-root/s2i

# Override image metadata for builder image.

mkdir -p /tmp/.s2i

cat > /tmp/.s2i/image_metadata.json << EOF
{
  "labels": [
    { "io.openshift.s2i.scripts-url": "image:///opt/app-root/s2i" }
  ]
}
EOF
```

This script moves the *assemble, run,* and *usage* scripts from before into the */opt/app-root/s2i* directory of the image. The */tmp/.s2i/image_metadata.json* file is then created, setting the `io.openshift.s2i.scripts-url` label to that directory.

When the S2I build process is run on these source files, the label information in the *image_metadata.json* file will be used to update the label on the final image created.

In addition to the *.s2i/bin/assemble* script, we also add *.s2i/bin/run*. In this we add:

```
#!/bin/bash

exec /opt/app-root/s2i/run
```

This will be set as the `CMD` used when the image is run.

If the normal pattern for an S2I builder were followed, this would invoke */opt/app-root/s2i/usage*. In this case the *run* script is being invoked instead. This means the resulting image can be run either as an S2I builder or as a standalone application image, with the static files being mounted into the container from a persistent volume.

To build the custom S2I image, you can run:

```
$ oc new-build --strategy=source --name simple-http-server \
  --code https://github.com/openshift-katacoda/simple-http-server \
  --image-stream python:2.7
```

Using an S2I builder and updating the image metadata in this way allows you to create new S2I builder images without needing to build the image from a `Dockerfile`.

The only restriction is that the build runs as a non-*root* user, and as such it is not possible to install additional operating system packages.

Summary

A Source-to-Image builder can typically be configured by passing environment variables through to the build or subsequent deployment of the application image created.

If you need more control over the build, you can override the *assemble* and *run* scripts by providing your own scripts in your application source code. The *run* script can also be overridden for a specific deployment of an application created using S2I, from a deployment configuration.

When an *assemble* script is provided with the application source code it is possible to update the image metadata for the container image created, so that if the image created is used as an S2I builder it will use a different set of S2I scripts than the original. Updating the image metadata in this way makes it possible to create your own custom S2I builder images without needing to use the Docker build strategy, using the Source build strategy instead.

## CHAPTER 10

Using Incremental and Chained Builds

When a Source-to-Image builder is used, the build phase is performed in a single step by the *assemble* script. One issue with this is that each build is distinct. This means that build artifacts generated by one build cannot be used for a subsequent build. As everything needs to be re-created each time, this can slow down build times.

Part of the reason it can be slow is that for each build it would be necessary to pull down third-party packages over the internet from a remote package repository. One way of speeding this up is to deploy a local caching proxy server through which downloads are routed. Downloading of the package will be sped up as the package can be provided by the cache, avoiding the need to download it from a remote package index each time.

Use of a local caching proxy server, though, will not eliminate the need to recompile a package that is only provided as source code, unless the cache also supports uploading of a precompiled package to the cache that the build process can use.

An alternative to using a local caching proxy server is to save build artifacts from a build in OpenShift and copy them across to subsequent builds so that they can be reused. In this chapter, you will learn how you can use incremental and chained builds to speed up build times by reusing the build artifacts of prior builds.

Faster Builds Using Caching

When you develop and deploy an application locally on your own computer system, you achieve faster build times by reusing artifacts from previous builds of your application. You do not, for example, need to download and install all of the third-party packages your application requires each time you deploy your application after a change. For a compiled programming language, build tools are often smart enough to know that certain code files do not need to be recompiled as the code change won't affect them.

When using an S2I builder, however, everything that may be required to build the application has to be done every time. This is because each build is run in a new container, starting with only the builder base image.

In the case of needing to download third-party packages from the internet, some time can be saved by using a local caching proxy server. Depending on the packaging system for the language being used, this could be a normal caching HTTP proxy, or it might be a special-purpose proxy cache. For Java this might be Nexus or Artifactory, and for Python it might be a Python Package Index (PyPi) mirror or proxy such as devpi-server. Such local caching proxies may not eliminate, though, the need to recompile code for packages each time.

OpenShift provides two mechanisms designed to try to reduce the time taken to run S2I builds of an application. These can be used to implement custom caching solutions, enabling the carryover of build artifacts from one build to the next or providing a local cache server for precompiled build artifacts. These two mechanisms are *incremental builds* and *chained builds*.

Using Incremental Builds

In Chapter 8 you learned how the S2I build process works. The first step in the process was to start up a container using the builder image and inject the application source code into the running container. The basis of incremental builds is that in addition to your application source code, a set of build artifacts recovered from a previous build is injected into the container at the same time.

For an S2I builder to support incremental builds, it must satisfy three requirements.

The first of these is that it must not discard build artifacts that could be carried over to a subsequent build. This can be an issue, as one goal when building an application image is to make the image as small as possible. Often intermediary build artifacts that could be used to speed up a subsequent build will be discarded.

The second is that the S2I builder must provide a script to extract the build artifacts from the image created by a previous build.

The third and final requirement is that the *assemble* script for an S2I builder must know to look for and use any build artifacts injected into the container for the new build.

Saving Artifacts from a Build

In order to extract build artifacts from the previous image produced by a build, the S2I builder must provide a *save-artifacts* script. This should be placed in the same directory as the *assemble* and *run* scripts. An example of a generic *save-artifacts* script is as follows:

```
#!/bin/bash

mkdir -p /opt/app-root/cache
echo "Incremental Build" > /opt/app-root/cache/README.txt

tar -C /opt/app-root -cf - cache
```

The output from the *save-artifacts* script should be a tar archive stream of the build artifacts. In this example the script expects that any build artifacts that are to be carried over to a subsequent build have been placed by the *assemble* script into the directory */opt/app-root/cache*.

If the */opt/app-root/cache* directory doesn't exist, the script first creates it. This is done to ensure we are always returning something from the script. The *README.txt* file is created as a marker file, as the S2I build process discards the output if all it contains is empty directories with no files.

Restoring the Build Artifacts

When the S2I build process is run and incremental build support is enabled, a temporary container will be started from the image produced by the previous build. The command run in this temporary container will be the *save-artifacts* script. The output will be captured and injected into the container for the new build, along with the application source code. The build artifacts will be placed in the container in the directory */tmp/artifacts*.

To restore the build artifacts the *assemble* script will check for the existence of the *cache* directory under */tmp/artifacts* and move it to a location where the subsequent build steps can use it:

```
if [ -d /tmp/artifacts/cache ]; then
    echo " -----> Restoring cache directory from incremental build."
    mv /tmp/artifacts/cache /opt/app-root/
fi
```

If the S2I builder normally discards build artifacts the *save-artifacts* script will have nothing to save away. In this case, the *assemble* script can use the existence of the */tmp/artifacts* directory to enable the retention of build artifacts.

Enabling Incremental Builds

To enable incremental builds for an existing build configuration, you must set the `spec.strategy.sourceStrategy.incremental` property of the build configuration to `true`.

To enable incremental builds on the sample blog site application from Chapter 6, you can use the `oc patch` command:

```
$ oc patch bc/blog --type=json --patch \
  '[{"op":"add",
     "path":"/spec/strategy/sourceStrategy/incremental",
     "value":true}]'
```

A new build should then be triggered:

```
$ oc start-build blog
```

In the case of the blog application, the Python S2I builder was used, which does not support incremental builds. Incremental build support was instead added by adding a suitable *save-artifacts* and *assemble* script wrapper to the application source code.

Because the Python S2I builder would normally not cache the third-party packages when they are downloaded and built, it was necessary to enable this, too. This was done by triggering the creation of the *cache* directory the first time the incremental build was done. The result was that the first incremental build still took the same amount of time, as there were no cached artifacts to use. It was only on subsequent builds that the speedup was realized:

```
$ oc get builds
NAME     TYPE    FROM         STATUS     STARTED         DURATION
blog-1   Source  Git@832a277  Complete   5 minutes ago   38s
blog-2   Source  Git@832a277  Complete   4 minutes ago   41s
blog-3   Source  Git@832a277  Complete   3 minutes ago   23s
blog-4   Source  Git@832a277  Complete   2 minutes ago   24s
```

The first build where the cached build artifacts were used was thus `blog-3`, after incremental builds had been enabled prior to `blog-2`. When the build artifacts were available, the build time was almost halved. How much improvement you will see will depend on the S2I builder being used, the application, and what types of build artifacts are being cached across builds.

Because incremental builds are dependent on the S2I builder *assemble* script including support, you will see no benefit if incremental builds are enabled when no support has been added. If using one of the S2I builders included with OpenShift, or one from a third party, ensure you check any documentation to see whether incremental build support is included and whether you need to make changes to your application code for it to work.

Using Chained Builds

Chained builds are similar to incremental builds in that files are copied across from an existing image. There are, however, two key differences when using chained builds.

The first is that instead of the files being copied from a previous build of the same image, they are copied from a separate image. This can be an image imported into the cluster or an image that has been built in the cluster. It is also possible to copy in files from more than one image at the same time.

The second is that instead of the files being copied to a fixed location in the image separate from the application source files, they will be merged with the application source files at a location you choose.

Using chained builds it is possible to set up a separate build configuration to prebuild artifacts into an image that is then used in multiple application images. Chained builds also allow a special build-time image to be used to generate an executable application, with the executable application then being copied into a smaller runtime image without the build tools and compilers.

The blog application we have been using for examples is implemented in the Python programming language. One mechanism used in Python to speed up build times is to precompile Python packages into Python *wheels*. These are files that contain the installed version of a Python package, including any compiled C extension modules.

Although Python wheels can be uploaded to PyPi, packages may not provide them for your platform when C extension modules are used.

To download and precompile a set of packages into Python wheels, an S2I builder can be used to create a Python wheelhouse.

A Python wheelhouse S2I builder that works for our blog application can be imported by running:

```
$ oc import-image openshiftkatacoda/python-wheelhouse --confirm
```

This can then be used to prebuild the Python wheels into an image:

```
$ oc new-build --name blog-wheelhouse \
    --image-stream python-wheelhouse \
    --code https://github.com/openshift-katacoda/blog-django-py
```

In this case we used the same source code repository as where the blog application source code resides. All that is being used from the repository is the list of packages from the *requirements.txt* file. We could have used a separate source code repository that built a larger set of packages and not just those required by the blog application. This could then be used instead of a local proxy server or cache such as devpi-server.

To create the chained build we need to use `oc new-build` to first create the build for the application. The `--source-image` option specifies the name of the image containing the prebuilt artifacts. The `--source-image-path` option indicates which directory in the source image should be copied into the application image when it's being built, and at what relative location in the application source code:

```
$ oc new-build --name blog \
    --image-stream python:3.5 \
    --code https://github.com/openshift-katacoda/blog-django-py \
    --source-image blog-wheelhouse \
    --source-image-path /opt/app-root/wheelhouse/.:.s2i/wheelhouse
```

When the build has finished, then deploy the image:

```
$ oc new-app --image-stream blog
oc expose svc/blog
```

When using chained builds, the S2I builder used to build the application image (or a custom *assemble* script in the application source code) needs to support the prebuilt artifacts being copied in. For the blog application, the Python S2I builder doesn't provide any support for this, and the custom *assemble* script handled setting the configuration. Now, the Python wheels copied in from the wheelhouse image will be used, instead of downloading and recompiling the Python packages.

The result for the blog application, when using a chained build rather than an incremental build, is an immediate speedup in build times:

```
$ oc get builds
NAME    TYPE    FROM        STATUS    STARTED        DURATION
blog-1  Source  Git@04599b1 Complete  3 minutes ago  24s
blog-2  Source  Git@04599b1 Complete  2 minutes ago  22s
```

The wheelhouse image used by the blog application will need to be rebuilt only when the list of Python packages needed changes or a newer version of a package is available. If the wheelhouse image is updated, the image triggers defined in the build configuration will automatically result in the blog application being rebuilt.

Summary

As a Source-to-Image builder starts over each time, building an application image may be slow. This can be due to the need to download third-party packages from an external package repository or to compiling source code each time a build occurs, even if the source code has not changed.

To speed up S2I builds, S2I builders can implement support for incremental or chained builds. These allow precompiled artifacts from a prior build of the image, or those from a completely separate build, to be used in a new build.

## CHAPTER 11

Webhooks and Build Automation

The support in OpenShift for the Docker and Source build strategies simplifies the build and deployment process, as OpenShift worries about the details of running the steps for you.

When the source code is contained in a hosted Git repository, OpenShift can also automatically trigger a rebuild and new deployment when the S2I builder image, or the base image used for a Docker build, has been updated. This is because it can pull down the last used source code from the Git repository whenever it needs to.

With what you have learned so far, any time you make changes to the source code you will currently still need to manually trigger a new build with the latest source code.

In order to completely automate your development workflow, in this chapter you will learn how to link your Git repository to OpenShift using a webhook. This will allow you to have a new build automatically started on code changes, each time you commit and push those changes to your Git repository.

Because you likely will want to use a private hosted Git repository, where access to your source code is only possible by first supplying appropriate access credentials, this chapter will also look at how to use OpenShift with a private hosted Git repository.

Using a Hosted Git Repository

You've seen how to set up the build and deployment of an application from source code, using the web console or `oc` command-line tool. The build can make use of a Source-to-Image builder, or the application can be built from a `Dockerfile`.

You also now how to manually trigger a new build of the application, from the description of the build configuration in the web console or by running the `oc start-build` command from the command line.

Except in the case of a binary input source build being used, the application source code will be pulled down from a master copy or branch in a separate Git repository hosting service. When the application source code can be pulled down in this way by OpenShift, it means that it can be rebuilt at any time, without a user needing to do anything. This allows us to start automating the end-to-end build and deployment process.

Accessing a Private Git Repository

The examples so far have used application source code hosted in a public Git repository. For your own application, you may want to use a private Git repository.

When using a private Git repository, secure access is achieved using either an SSH or HTTPS connection, and you need to provide access credentials.

Because the access credentials are the key to your Git repository and need to be stored inside OpenShift, it is important to use credentials for a user account that has limited rights to work on the Git repository and that isn't used for any other purpose. For an SSH connection, you should not use your primary identity key.

To create a separate SSH key pair for use by OpenShift when accessing the repository, run the `ssh-keygen` command. Save the result into a file named for the repository it will be used with:

```
$ ssh-keygen -f ~/.ssh/github-blog-sshauth
```

When asked to supply a passphrase, leave it empty as OpenShift cannot use an SSH key that requires a passphrase.

The `ssh-keygen` command will create two files. The private key file will use the name supplied and the public key file will have the same basename but with a *.pub* extension added to the end.

You should configure your Git repository hosting service to use the public key. If using GitHub or GitLab, this is called a *deploy key*. If using Bitbucket it is called an *access key*. Ensure when adding the key that it is granted read-only access to the repository. This means OpenShift will be able to pull down the source code to do the build, but cannot make changes to the hosted Git repository.

Having set up the Git repository hosting service with the public key, you are ready to add the private key into OpenShift and configure OpenShift to use it for your application.

Create a secret in OpenShift to hold the private key:

```
$ oc secrets new-sshauth github-blog-sshauth \
  --ssh-privatekey=$HOME/.ssh/github-blog-sshauth
```

Grant the `builder` service account access to the secret, so it can be used when pulling down the source code to build the application:

```
$ oc secrets link builder github-blog-sshauth
```

Finally, add an annotation to the secret to identify the source code repository it is for:

```
$ oc annotate secret/github-blog-sshauth \
  'build.openshift.io/source-secret-match-uri-1=\
  ssh://github.com/openshift-katacoda/blog-django-py.git'
```

To create the application, use the SSH URI instead of the HTTPS URI:

```
$ oc new-app --name blog --image-stream python \
  --code git@github.com:openshift-katacoda/blog-django-py.git
```

Because the annotation was added to the secret, the build will automatically associate use of the repository with that secret and use the access credentials when pulling down the application source code.

If the Git repository hosting service being used does not support setting up SSH access keys, you can instead use basic authentication over HTTPS. This can use application access tokens if supported by the Git repository hosting service.

If you intend to use an HTTPS connection to interact with your Git repository, to create a secret for your credentials, use the command:

```
$ oc secrets new-basicauth github-blog-basicauth --username <username> --prompt
```

Replace *<username>* with the username used when accessing the Git repository. The `--prompt` option ensures that you are prompted to enter the user password or application access token.

Grant the *builder* service account access to the secret and annotate it with details of the repository to be accessed.

Adding the annotation to the secret provides for automatic linking of access credentials to a build. If necessary, you can also edit an existing build configuration and set the `spec.source.sourceSecret.name` property to the name of the secret holding the access credentials.

If using OpenShift 3.7 or later, in place of adding the annotation to the secret, you can instead supply the name of the source secret for the private Git repository to the `oc new-app` or `oc new-build` command when run, by using the `--source-secret` option.

Adding a Repository Webhook

A webhook (also known as a user-defined HTTP callback) is a way for an application to notify another application of a change.

All major Git repository hosting services support generating a callback via a webhook when a new set of source code changes is pushed to the hosted Git repository. Open-Shift accepts a callback via a webhook as a means to trigger a new build.

By configuring the Git repository hosting service with the details of the URL Open-Shift accepts for the callback, you can fully automate your development workflow, such that committing and pushing the changes back to your hosted Git repository will start the new build and deployment.

 A webhook can only be used with an OpenShift cluster that is visible to the Git repository hosting service. You cannot use a webhook when using Minishift or oc cluster up, as these can be seen only from the computer system they are running on.

To determine the URL for the webhook callback, run the oc describe command on the build configuration:

```
$ oc describe bc/blog
Name:          blog
Namespace:     myproject
Created:       29 hours ago
Labels:        app=blog
Annotations:   openshift.io/generated-by=OpenShiftNewApp
Latest Version: 1

Strategy:      Source
URL:           https://github.com/openshift-katacoda/blog-django-py
From Image:    ImageStreamTag openshift/python:3.5
Output to:     ImageStreamTag blog:latest

Build Run Policy:    Serial
Triggered by:        Config, ImageChange
Webhook GitHub:
     URL:     https://api.pro-us-east-1.openshift.com:443/oapi/v1/namespaces/
myproject/buildconfigs/blog/webhooks/3dhkEZGRlHD18XKbK_0e/github

Build   Status            Duration       Creation Time
blog-1  complete   47s    2017-10-23 16:23:47 +1100 AEDT

Events: <none>
```

Different URLs are used for GitHub, GitLab, and Bitbucket. If you need to regenerate the webhook URL with a new secret token, or a webhook URL does not appear for the Git hosting service you are using, you can run the command `oc set triggers` with the build configuration name as an argument, and pass the option `--from-github`, `--from-gitlab`, or `--from-bitbucket` as appropriate. Rerun `oc describe` on the build configuration to view the new webhook URL.

Use the URL when configuring the Git repository hosting service to trigger the webhook when a push event occurs for your Git repository. When adding the webhook callback to the Git repository hosting service, ensure that the content type for the generated HTTP callback is `application/json`.

Customized Build Triggers

In addition to supporting special webhook callbacks for the major Git repository hosting services, a generic webhook callback can also be used to trigger a new build. This can be used by any service that is capable of making a web request. The callback could, for example, be triggered by the successful completion of tests run on the application source code by a third party.

In other words, rather than the Git repository hosting service triggering OpenShift to run a build, it would notify a third-party testing service to run tests on the code first. OpenShift would then only go on to build and deploy the code if the tests passed.

The URL for the generic webhook can be found by running `oc describe` on the build configuration. If a generic webhook URL hasn't been set up for the build configuration, run `oc set triggers` on the build configuration with the `--from-webhook` option.

When you're using a generic webhook, passing additional build-time environment variables as part of the webhook request body is also supported. This approach can be used to customize how the application is built. For further details on passing environment variables, see the OpenShift documentation on generic webhooks (*http://bit.ly/2EGPISN*).

 Chapter 6 looked at another method for integrating tests into the workflow, by running tests within the application image after it has been built. The build would be marked as successful only if those tests had passed.

Summary

OpenShift builds on top of Kubernetes a build system that implements a PaaS layer. This build system can be used to build applications from source code using a Source-to-Image builder or a set of instructions provided in a `Dockerfile`.

When building from application source code, the files can be pulled from a hosted Git repository. This may be a public or private Git repository. Input for builds can also be uploaded for a single build from a local directory on your own system.

When using a hosted Git repository, you can configure a webhook callback to be fired whenever code changes are pushed up to the Git repository. This can be used to trigger a new build and deployment of the application in OpenShift. If using a separate test server, the webhook could instead trigger a test suite to be run first, with the success of the tests triggering the build and deployment using a separate webhook.

## CHAPTER 12

Configuration and Secrets

Best practice when developing applications is to keep the source code in a version control system such as Git. This ensures that you can roll back to a previous version of the source code. Although default configuration settings are best also kept under version control with your application source code, secret information such as database access credentials or SSH keys should be stored separately.

Such secret information, along with separate configuration settings that customize the application defaults, is not part of the application source code but needs to be available to the application when it is run within a container. To facilitate this, OpenShift can store configuration and secrets as resources within a project, with them being added to the container when the deployment occurs.

The simplest way of storing separate configuration is to add definitions of environment variables to be set within a container as part of a build or deployment configuration. Examples of setting environment variables in this way were demonstrated in previous chapters showing deployment of applications from a pre-existing image and source code.

In this chapter you will learn more about using environment variables, as well as the storage and use of secrets. This will include how using config maps enables configuration to be defined in one place and referenced in more than one build or deployment configuration to avoid duplication. In addition to consuming configuration and secrets as environment variables, how to map these into a container so they are available as a file will also be covered.

Passing Environment Variables

Environment variables can be defined when building an image from source code or in any situation where a container is being run.

The querying, addition, or removal of environment variables in a build or deployment configuration is handled by the oc set env command.

To list the names and values of the environment variables run the oc set env command, passing the name of the resource object as an argument and using the --list option:

```
$ oc set env dc/blog --list
# deploymentconfigs blog, container blog
DATABASE_URL=postgres://user145c30ca:EbAYDR1sJsvW@blog-db:5432/blog
```

To add a new environment variable pass the name of the environment variable and its value, separated by =:

```
$ oc set env dc/blog BLOG_BANNER_COLOR=blue
```

This will overwrite any existing value if the environment variable has already been set. You can use --overwrite=false to have the update fail if the environment variable exists but with a different value.

To set more than one environment variable at the same time, list them one after another with a space between:

```
$ oc set env dc/blog BLOG_BANNER_COLOR=blue BLOG_SITE_NAME="My Blog"
```

If you have the environment variables to be set in a file or want to set them from your local environment, you can pipe them into the oc set env command, passing a - to indicate it should read them from the pipe:

```
$ env | grep '^AWS_' | oc set env dc/blog -
```

Any time you are setting the value of an environment variable, if you need to compose the value from other environment variables that are already being set, you can use $(<VARNAME>) in the value. Ensure you surround the argument with single quotes when setting it from the command line, to avoid the local shell trying to interpret the value:

```
$ oc set env dc/blog \
DATABASE_USERNAME=user145c30ca \
DATABASE_PASSWORD=EbAYDR1sJsvW \
DATABASE_URL='postgres://$(DATABASE_USERNAME):$(DATABASE_PASSWORD)@blog-db/blog'
```

If you need the value to include the literal string of form $(<VARNAME>), use $$(<VARNAME>) to prevent it from being interpreted. The result will be passed through as $(<VARNAME>).

To delete an environment variable, instead of using the name of the variable followed by = and the value, use the name of the variable followed by -:

```
$ oc set env dc/blog BLOG_BANNER_COLOR-
```

When updating a deployment configuration, by default these commands will be applied to all containers in the pod definition. If you only want the operation to apply to a single container, you can name the container using the `--container` option.

Working with Configuration Files

Environment variables are the easiest mechanism to use for injecting configuration information into a container. Configuration passed using environment variables is, though, restricted to being in the form of simple key/value pairs. This method is not well suited for passing more complex structured data to applications, such as JSON, YAML, XML, or INI-formatted configuration files.

For working with more complex data, OpenShift provides the `configmap` resource type. This also provides the ability to store keyed data, but the data values can be more complex. In addition to being able to be passed into a container via environment variables, configuration held in a config map can be made available in a container as a file, making this approach suitable for use with traditional configuration files.

To create a config map you can use `oc create configmap`, or `oc create` with a JSON/YAML resource definition for the config map.

If you only need to store simple key/value pairs, you can create the config map by running `oc create configmap` and passing the `--from-literal` option along with the names and values for the settings:

```
oc create configmap blog-settings \
    --from-literal BLOG_BANNER_COLOR=blue \
    --from-literal BLOG_SITE_NAME="My Blog"
```

You can see the definition of the config map by querying the resource created using `oc get -o json`. The key parts of the definition needed to reproduce it are:

```
{
    "apiVersion": "v1",
    "kind": "ConfigMap",
    "metadata": {
        "name": "blog-settings"
    },
    "data": {
        "BLOG_BANNER_COLOR": "blue",
        "BLOG_SITE_NAME": "My Blog"
    }
}
```

If you were to take this definition and save it as *blog-settings-configmap.json*, you could also load it by running:

```
$ oc create -f blog-settings-configmap.json
```

When a config map is created, it is not associated with any application. To pass the settings in this config map as environment variables in a deployment configuration, you need to run the extra step of:

```
$ oc set env dc/blog --from configmap/blog-settings
```

The result of running oc set env on the deployment configuration with the --list option will now be:

```
# deploymentconfigs blog, container blog
# BLOG_BANNER_COLOR from configmap blog-settings, key BLOG_BANNER_COLOR
# BLOG_SITE_NAME from configmap blog-settings, key BLOG_SITE_NAME
```

The environment variables will be set as before, but rather than being stored in the deployment configuration, they are referenced from the config map. When the container is started, the value for each environment variable will be copied from the config map.

You can associate the same config map with any other applications that require it. This means you can use the config map to keep configuration in one place, rather than needing to duplicate it in each build or deployment configuration.

For more complicated data, you can create the config map using a file as input. Create a file called *blog.json* containing:

```
{
    "BLOG_BANNER_COLOR": "blue",
    "BLOG_SITE_NAME": "My Blog"
}
```

To create the config map, instead of using --from-literal, use --from-file:

```
$ oc create configmap blog-settings-file --from-file blog.json
```

Running oc describe on the config map created, the result is:

```
$ oc describe configmap/blog-settings-file
Name:          blog-settings-file
Namespace:     myproject
Labels:        <none>
Annotations:   <none>

Data
====
blog.json:
----
{
    "BLOG_BANNER_COLOR": "blue",
    "BLOG_SITE_NAME": "My Blog"
}
```

The name of the file is used as the key. If it were necessary for the key to be different from the name of the file used as input, you would use *<key>*=blog.json as the argument to the --from-file option, replacing *key* with the name you want to use.

To mount a config map into a container as a set of files, run:

```
$ oc set volume dc/blog --add --configmap-name blog-settings-file \
  --mount-path=/opt/app-root/src/settings
```

This will result in files being created in the directory specified by the --mount-path option, where the names of the files created correspond to the keys, and the contents of the files are the values associated with those keys.

 If the path specified by --mount-path is a directory that contains existing files, those files will be hidden from view and no longer accessible.

If you have more than one configuration file, you can add them all to one config map. This can be done by passing more than one --from-file option to oc create configmap. Alternatively, if the files are all in the same directory by themselves, pass the path of the directory to --from-file. Each file in the directory will be added under a separate key.

To change a config map you can use oc edit on it, or you can save the current resource definition to a file using oc get -o json or oc get -o yaml, edit the definition in the file, and replace the original by running oc replace -f with the file as the argument.

When you edit the definition of a config map, the changes will be automatically reflected in the file mounted from the config map in any running containers. This will not be instantaneous, with the changes taking up to a minute or more to appear depending on how the OpenShift cluster is configured. If an application automatically detects changes to the configuration file and rereads it, the changes will be used straightaway, without needing to redeploy the application.

If the config map is used to set environment variables, the application will not be automatically redeployed. You will need to force a redeployment with the updated values by running oc deploy --latest on the deployment configuration.

Handling of Secret Information

Secrets such as database credentials can be stored in a config map and passed to an application using environment variables or in a configuration file. Because security of secrets is important, OpenShift provides an alternative resource type for handling secret data called a secret.

A generic secret works the same as a config map, but OpenShift manages them internally in a more secure manner. This includes data volumes for secrets being backed by temporary file-storage facilities (tmpfs) and never coming to rest on a node. Secrets can also only be accessed by service accounts that need them, or to which access has been explicitly granted.

To create a generic secret you can use oc create secret generic, or oc create -f with a JSON/YAML resource definition for the secret.

If you only need to store simple key/value pairs, you can create the secret by running oc create secret generic and passing the --from-literal option along with the names and values for the settings:

```
$ oc create secret generic blog-secrets \
  --from-literal DATABASE_USERNAME=user145c30ca \
  --from-literal DATABASE_PASSWORD=EbAYDR1sJsvW
```

You can see the definition of the secret by querying the resource created using oc get -o json. The key parts of the definition needed to reproduce it are:

```
{
    "apiVersion": "v1",
    "kind": "Secret",
    "metadata": {
        "name": "blog-secrets"
    },
    "data": {
        "DATABASE_USERNAME": "dXNlcjE0NWMzMGNh",
        "DATABASE_PASSWORD": "RWJBWURSMXNKc3ZX"

    }
}
```

You will note that the value for each key under data has been obfuscated by applying base64 encoding. If you are creating the resource definition yourself, you will need to do the encoding yourself when adding the values. You can create the obfuscated values using the Unix base64 command.

For convenience, especially when using a secret in a template definition, you can supply the values as clear text, as long as you add them under the stringData field rather than the data field:

```
{
    "apiVersion": "v1",
    "kind": "Secret",
    "metadata": {
        "name": "blog-secrets"
    },
```

```
    "stringData": {
      "DATABASE_USERNAME": "user145c30ca",
      "DATABASE_PASSWORD": "EbAYDR1sJsvW"
    }
  }
```

Even when created in this way, when queried back the secret will always show the data field with values obfuscated. The Unix `base64` command can be used to deobfuscate the values, and an option also exists to reveal the deobfuscated values if viewing the secret through the web console.

To pass the settings in this secret as environment variables in a deployment configuration, you need to run the extra step of:

```
$ oc set env dc/blog --from secret/blog-secrets
```

The result of running `oc set env` on the deployment configuration with the `--list` option will now be:

```
# deploymentconfigs blog, container blog
# DATABASE_USERNAME from secret blog-secrets, key DATABASE_USERNAME
# DATABASE_PASSWORD from secret blog-secrets, key DATABASE_PASSWORD
```

To create the secret using a file, instead of using `--from-literal` use `--from-file`, overriding the key used for the value as necessary:

```
$ oc create secret generic blog-webdav-users
--from-file .htdigest=webdav.htdigest
```

To mount the secret, use `oc set volume`, using the `--secret-name` option to identify the secret to use:

```
$ oc set volume dc/blog --add --secret-name blog-webdav-users \
    --mount-path=/opt/app-root/secrets/webdav
```

To change a secret you can use `oc edit` on it, or you can save the current resource definition to a file using `oc get -o json` or `oc get -o yaml`, edit the definition in the file, and replace the original by running `oc apply -f` with the file as the argument.

Deleting Configuration and Secrets

When you create config maps or secrets they are created independent from any existing build or deployment configuration and are not associated with a specific application. If you want to associate them with a specific application in order to track them, you will need to add a label to them explicitly. This can be done using the `oc label` command:

```
$ oc label secrets/blog-secrets app=blog
```

When you delete an application using `oc delete all` and a label selector, any config maps or secrets to which that label has been applied will not be deleted. This is because `all` does not include resource objects of type `configmap` and `secret` in the selection.

To delete all resource objects for an application using a label selector, including `secret` and `configmap` object types, use:

```
$ oc delete all,configmap,secret --selector app=blog
```

Summary

Configuration can be passed to a build or a running container using environment variables. The environment variables are set in the build or deployment configuration.

In the case of a deployment, it is also possible to define a config map or secret. These can hold key/value pairs that can be used to populate environment variables in a deployment configuration or mounted as files into a running container.

A secret works the same way as a config map but provides extra guarantees as to how it is managed by OpenShift. This includes controlling who can access a secret and ensuring that a secret is never stored to disk on the node where applications are run.

## CHAPTER 13

Services, Networking, and Routing

When you deploy an application, whether it is a web application or a database, you need it to be accessible so other application components, or users, can access it. You want to be able to control, though, who or what can access it.

In most cases, when you deploy an application in OpenShift, it will be accessible only to other application components running in the same project. In order to make a web application visible so that users outside the OpenShift cluster can access it, you need to create a route. The creation of a *route* gives your web application a public URL by which users can access it.

In this chapter you will learn about the relationship between containers and pods, how your application can access other applications running in the same or a different project, and how you can expose your application to external users.

Containers and Pods

Your application, when deployed, is run within a *container*. The container isolates your application from other applications. From within the container, your application can see only processes that are a part of the same deployed application. It cannot see the processes of applications running in other containers.

When containers are run directly on a host, although applications are isolated from each other, all the containers will normally share the same IP address and port namespace.

This means that if you want to run multiple instances of the same web application, all wanting to use the same listener port for accepting web requests, they will conflict with each other.

For this reason, when your application is run within OpenShift, the container is further encapsulated in what is called a *pod*.

A pod is a group of containers with shared storage and network resources. The containers in a pod are always co-located and co-scheduled, and run in a shared context.

Containers within a pod share an IP address and port namespace, and can find each other via localhost. They can also communicate with each other using local inter-process communication (IPC) mechanisms like SystemV semaphores or POSIX shared memory. Containers in different pods have distinct IP addresses and cannot communicate using local IPC mechanisms.

Each pod having its own IP address and port namespace means that multiple instances of an application, all wanting to use the same listener port for accepting web requests, can be run on the same host, without your needing to override what port each is using. A pod in that respect behaves as if it were its own host.

To see a list of all pods within a project, you can run the `oc get pods` command. If you wish to see more information on a pod, including the IP address of the pod and details of each container running in the pod, run `oc describe pod`, passing the name of the pod as the argument.

It is not possible from outside a container to see what processes are running in it. In order to see what is running in a container, you can use `oc rsh` to start an interactive terminal session within the container. Provided the application image bundles the required Unix commands, you can interact with the processes from the terminal session, in the same way as you would if they were running on your own host. You can use Unix commands such as `ps` or `top` to list the processes that are running.

Services and Endpoints

Each pod has a distinct IP address. From any application running in the same project, you can connect to another pod using its IP address on the port the application that is running in that pod is using.

 In order to be able to accept connections on a port from outside the pod, an application should bind to the network address 0.0.0.0 and not 127.0.0.1 or localhost.

Using the direct IP address of a pod when connecting to it is not recommended. This is because the IP addresses are not permanent and can change if a pod is killed and replaced with an instance of the application running in a new pod.

If you have multiple instances of an application, they will each run in a separate pod. These may be on the same node, or a different node in the OpenShift cluster. Each instance will have a separate IP address.

In order to have a single permanent IP address that can be used to connect to any instance of the application and to load-balance connections between the instances of the application, OpenShift provides a service abstraction. If you use `oc new-app` or the web console to deploy an application from a pre-existing image, or one built from your source code, a `service` resource object will be created for you automatically.

To see a list of both the pods and services for an application, you can run `oc get pods,services` and provide a label selector which matches that used by the application:

```
$ oc get pods,services --selector app=blog
NAME                READY   STATUS    RESTARTS   AGE
po/blog-2-sxbpd     1/1     Running   0          1m
po/blog-2-ww5ck     1/1     Running   0          1m


NAME         CLUSTER-IP      EXTERNAL-IP   PORT(S)    AGE
svc/blog     172.30.229.46   <none>        8080/TCP   2m
```

The entry for the service will display the permanent IP address that can be used to connect to the application. When there are multiple instances of the application, the instance you connect to will be random.

To see a list of the pod IP addresses associated with a service, you can use the `oc get endpoints` command:

```
$ oc get endpoints blog
NAME    ENDPOINTS                            AGE
blog    172.17.0.10:8080,172.17.0.8:8080     2m
```

Although the IP address of the service remains the same for the life of the application, you cannot determine what IP address will be used in advance.

If you were deploying an application directly to a host, to avoid users of the application having to know an IP address, you would register the IP address against a hostname within a DNS server. When you use OpenShift and a service is created, this will be done for you, with the IP address being registered in a DNS server internal to the OpenShift cluster and the hostname used matching the name of the service.

In this example, rather than a client application running in the same project needing to use the IP address, it would be able to use the hostname `blog` to connect to the application.

The registration of the IP address in the DNS server means that client applications can be coded to use a fixed hostname, and the deployed backend application or database need only use the same name when it is created.

Alternatively, you could pass the hostname for the backend application or database to the client application using an environment variable, or in a configuration file mounted into the container for the client application using a config map or secret.

Connecting Between Projects

When using the unqualified name of the service for an application as the hostname, the name will only be able to be resolved from within the project where the application is deployed. If you need to be able to access a backend application or database from a different project, you will need to use a qualified hostname that incorporates the name of the project.

The format for the fully qualified hostname is:

```
<service-name>.<project-name>.svc.cluster.local
```

For example, if the service name is `blog` and it's deployed in the project `myproject`, the fully qualified hostname will be `blog.myproject.svc.cluster.local`.

As an installation of OpenShift is by default provisioned as multitenant, and applications in one project cannot see any applications deployed in different projects, before you can attempt to make connections directly from one project to another you will need to enable access. To open up access between projects you can use the `oc adm pod-network` command.

 If you are using Minishift or `oc cluster up`, these do not come with the multitenant network overlay enabled. This means you will actually be able to make connections across projects without needing to do anything.

If you require this ability, check out the OpenShift documentation on managing networks (*https://docs.openshift.org/latest/admin_guide/managing_networking.html*).

Creating External Routes

Neither the direct IP address of a pod or service nor the hostname for a service can be used to access an application from outside the OpenShift cluster. In order for a web application to be public and accessible from outside the OpenShift cluster, you will need to create a route.

To expose a service for a web application so it can be accessed externally by a user, you can run the `oc expose service` command, passing the name of the service as an additional argument:

```
$ oc expose service/blog
route "blog" exposed
```

When a route is created, OpenShift will by default assign your application a unique hostname by which it can be accessed from outside the OpenShift cluster. You can see the details of the route created by running oc describe on the route:

```
$ oc describe route/blog
Name:              blog
Namespace:         myproject
Created:           5 minutes ago
Labels:            app=blog
Annotations:       openshift.io/host.generated=true
Requested Host:    blog-myproject.b9ad.pro-us-east-1.openshiftapps.com
                     exposed on router router 5 minutes ago
Path:              <none>
TLS Termination:   <none>
Insecure Policy:   <none>
Endpoint Port:     8080-tcp

Service:     blog
Weight:      100 (100%)
Endpoints:   172.17.0.4:8080
```

If you have your own custom hostname, you can use it rather than relying on the assigned hostname. This can be done by passing the hostname to oc expose using the --hostname option.

When using a custom hostname, you will need to have control over the DNS servers for the domain name. You will then need to create a CNAME record in the DNS server configuration for the hostname and point it at the hostname of the inbound router of the OpenShift cluster.

If you can't determine the hostname of the inbound router, you can usually use as the target of the CNAME any hostname value that would fall within the wildcard subdomain used by the OpenShift cluster for generated hostnames.

For the preceding example, where the assigned hostname was:

```
blog-myproject.b9ad.pro-us-east-1.openshiftapps.com
```

you could, as the target of the CNAME record, use:

```
myproject.b9ad.pro-us-east-1.openshiftapps.com
```

Where you have multiple instances of an application and a route is created, OpenShift will automatically configure routing so that traffic is distributed between the instances.

Sticky sessions will be used so that traffic from the same client will be preferentially routed back to the same instance.

Using Secure Connections

The route created using oc expose only supports requests using the HTTP protocol. It cannot be used to expose a database service using a non-HTTP protocol.

In the case of HTTP traffic, if you want clients to use a secure connection, you will need to create the route using oc create route instead of using oc expose.

Three types of secured routes are supported:

edge

> The secure connection is terminated by the router, with the router proxying the connection to the application using an insecure connection over the internal cluster network. If not supplying your own hostname and SSL certificate, the SSL certificate of the OpenShift cluster will be used. Although an insecure connection is used internally, the traffic is not visible to other users of the cluster.

passthrough

> The router will proxy the secure connection directly through to the application. The application must be able to accept a secure connection and be configured with the appropriate SSL certificate. Provided that the client supports Server Name Identification (SNI) over a Transport Layer Security (TLS) connection, this can be used to allow access to an application using non-HTTP protocols.

reencrypt

> The secure connection is terminated by the router, with the router re-encrypting traffic when proxying the connection to the application. If not supplying your own hostname and SSL certificate, the SSL certificate of the OpenShift cluster will be used for the initial inbound connection. For the connection from the router to the application, the application must be able to accept a secure connection and be configured with the appropriate SSL certificate used for the re-encrypted connection.

To create a secure connection using edge termination, where the hostname assigned by OpenShift is used, run the command:

```
$ oc create route edge blog-secure --service blog
```

If you have already created a route using oc expose for the insecure connection, the name supplied for the route must be different. In this example the name of the route was given as blog-secure.

Rather than creating separate routes for the insecure and secure connections, you can create a single route that covers both cases by specifying how the insecure connection should be handled.

If you want to allow a web application to accept HTTP requests via both insecure and secure connections, run:

```
$ oc create route edge blog --service blog --insecure-policy Allow
```

If you want users who attempt to use an insecure connection to be redirected so that a secure connection is used, run:

```
$ oc create route edge blog --service blog --insecure-policy Redirect
```

If using your own custom hostname, you can supply it using the `--hostname` option. You will need to supply the SSL certificate files using the `--key`, `--cert`, and `--ca-cert` options.

For a much deeper discussion of all the routing features OpenShift provides, including using `passthrough` and `reencrypt` secure routes, see the OpenShift architecture documentation on routes (*http://bit.ly/2H7OUTG*).

Internal and External Ports

When hosting an application using OpenShift, the user ID that a container runs as will be assigned based on which project it is running in. Containers are not allowed to run as the *root* user by default. Because containers do not run as the *root* user, they will not be able to use privileged port numbers below 1024. A web application would not, for example, be able to use the standard port 80 used for HTTP.

Images designed not to require running as *root* will use a higher port number. For web applications it is typical to use port 8080 instead of port 80. You can see what ports a service is advertised as using by running `oc get services`. From within the OpenShift cluster, when you access a pod directly via the IP address, or via the service using the IP address or hostname, you would use this port number.

If you expose a service externally using a route, an external user would instead use the standard port 80 for HTTP requests, or port 443 for HTTP requests over a secure connection. The routing layer will always accept requests via the standard ports and, when proxying the requests to the application, will map those to the internal port numbers.

The port used when routing an HTTP request is dictated by what port the image advertises itself as using and which was added to the service. If there is more than one port advertised by the image, the first is used. If this is the wrong port, you can override what port will be used by passing the `--port` option to `oc expose service` or `oc create route`.

Exposing Non-HTTP Services

Exposing a service via a route is only useful if you are running an HTTP-based service or a service that can terminate a secure connection, with the client supporting SNI over a secure connection using TLS.

If you wish to expose a different type of service, you have two choices.

First, you could dedicate a new public IP address for the service and configure network routing to pass connections to any port on that address through to the IP address of the internal service. If you have multiple services using the same port, you would need to dedicate a separate public IP address for each.

Alternatively, a dedicated port on the gateway host for the cluster could be assigned to the service. Any connections on this port would be routed through to a port on the internal service. Assigning a specific port to the service like this would result in the port being reserved on each node in the cluster, even though it would only be in use on one node at a time. If it were a standard port, you would not be able to use it for any other services.

Both these methods require additional setup to be performed by the cluster admin. For further information, check out the OpenShift documentation on getting traffic into a cluster on non standard ports (*http://bit.ly/2EJ2vDY*).

Local Port Forwarding

If the reason you want to expose a non-HTTP–based service is to allow temporary access to permit debugging of an application, loading of data, or administration, a service can be temporarily exposed to a local machine using port forwarding.

To use port forwarding, you need to identify a specific pod that you want to communicate with. You cannot use port forwarding to expose an application via the service. Use `oc get pods` with an appropriate label selector to identify the pod for the application:

```
$ oc get pods --selector name=postgresql
NAME                 READY   STATUS    RESTARTS   AGE
postgresql-1-8cng2   1/1     Running   0          5m
```

You can then run `oc port-forward` with the name of the pod and the port on the container you wish to connect to:

```
$ oc port-forward postgresql-1-8cng2 5432
Forwarding from 127.0.0.1:5432 -> 5432
Forwarding from [::1]:5432 -> 5432
```

The remote port will be exposed locally using the same port number. If the port number is already in use on the local machine, you can specify a different local port to use:

```
$ oc port-forward postgresql-1-8cng2 15432:5432
Forwarding from 127.0.0.1:15432 -> 5432
Forwarding from [::1]:15432 -> 5432
```

You can also have oc port-forward select a local port for you:

```
$ oc port-forward postgresql-1-8cng2 :5432
Forwarding from 127.0.0.1:48888 -> 5432
Forwarding from [::1]:48888 -> 5432
```

The oc port-forward command will run in the foreground until it is killed or the connection is lost. While the connection is active you can run a client program locally, connecting to the forwarded port on 127.0.0.1, with the connection being proxied through to the remote application:

```
$ psql sampledb username --host=127.0.0.1 --port=48888
Handling connection for 5432
psql (9.2.18, server 9.5.4)
Type "help" for help.

sampledb=>
```

Summary

When an application is deployed to OpenShift, by default, it will be accessible only within the OpenShift cluster. You can access the application from within the cluster using an internal hostname derived from the service name of the application.

When there are multiple instances of the application, connecting to the application will result in the connection being routed through to one of the pods that is running the application.

If you need to make an HTTP web service available to users outside the OpenShift cluster, you can expose it by creating a route. Creation of the route will result in OpenShift automatically reconfiguring the routing layer for you. You can expose a web application via the HTTP protocol or as HTTPS over a secure connection. OpenShift can provide an external hostname for you, or you can use your own custom hostname.

Services can also be exposed on a dedicated IP address or port, or temporarily to your own local system using port forwarding.

## CHAPTER 14

Working with Persistent Storage

When an application is run inside a container, it has access to its own filesystem. This contains a copy of the operating system files from the image, any application server or language runtime files, as well as the source code or compiled binary for the application being run.

When the application is running, it can write files to any part of the filesystem it has permission to write to, but when the container is stopped, any changes made will be lost. This is because the local container filesystem is *ephemeral*.

In order to preserve data created by an application across restarts of the application, or share dynamic data between instances of an application, *persistent storage* is required. This may be persistent storage that is attached directly to a container the application is running in, or persistent storage attached to a separate database running in OpenShift that the application is using.

In this chapter, you will learn about persistent storage provided by OpenShift, how to make a persistent volume claim, and how to mount the persistent volume into the container for an application.

Types of Persistent Storage

When an OpenShift cluster is set up, it will be configured for persistent storage by the cluster admin. The persistent volumes available may be pre-allocated from fixed storage, or a dynamic storage provisioner can be set up with persistent volumes being allocated on demand from a persistent storage provider.

OpenShift supports a number of underlying storage technologies including NFS, GlusterFS, Ceph RBD, OpenStack Cinder, AWS Elastic Block Storage, GCE Persistent Storage, Azure Disk, Azure File, iSCSI, Fibre Channel, and VMware vSphere.

When volumes are declared, they can be associated with a storage class indicating the type of technology used or other attributes, such as the performance of the disk. When requesting storage you can, if necessary, indicate that a persistent volume with a particular storage class is required.

The type of storage technology used will also dictate what access modes are supported and how the persistent volumes can be used.

Access modes for persistent storage are:

ReadWriteOnce *(RWO)*
> The volume can be mounted as read/write by a single node.

ReadOnlyMany *(ROX)*
> The volume can be mounted as read-only by many nodes.

ReadWriteMany *(RWX)*
> The volume can be mounted as read/write by many nodes.

For additional information see the OpenShift documentation for storage classes (*http://bit.ly/2EJKaXG*) and access modes (*http://bit.ly/2HAUYVC*).

If you are a cluster admin, you can view what persistent volumes have been predefined, including the access modes and storage classes, by running the command oc get pv. This information isn't accessible to a non-admin user of the OpenShift cluster, so you will need to ask the cluster admin what is available or, if using a hosted OpenShift service, check the documentation from the service provider.

It is possible that persistent storage available in an OpenShift cluster will not support all access modes. If the only supported access mode is ReadWriteOnce, this will limit how you can use persistent storage.

In the case of persistent storage with an access mode of ReadWriteOnce, you cannot use it with a scaled application and you will not be able to use rolling deployments. This is because a persistent volume supporting only that access mode can be mounted against only one node in the OpenShift cluster at any one time. When you scale an application, you are not guaranteed that all instances will run on the same node. In the case of a rolling deployment, even if the replica count is set to one instance, a new instance of the application will be started before the existing one is shut down. This presents the same problem as when an application is scaled up.

The topic of deployment strategies and how to change the deployment strategy used will be covered in Chapter 17.

Claiming a Persistent Volume

When you need persistent storage for an application, you need to make a *persistent volume claim*. When making the claim, you must specify the size of the persistent volume you want. You can optionally also specify the access mode you need the persistent volume to support. If not supplied, the access mode will default to ReadWriteOnce.

To make a persistent volume claim and mount the persistent volume against each instance of your application, you can use the oc set volume --add command. You must supply a directory path to use as the mount path for the persistent volume in the container. You can optionally specify a name for the persistent volume claim and a name to identify the volume mount in the deployment configuration. For example:

```
$ oc set volume dc/blog --add \
  --type=pvc --claim-size=1Gi --claim-mode=ReadWriteOnce \
  --claim-name blog-data --name data --mount-path /opt/app-root/src/media
persistentvolumeclaims/blog-data
deploymentconfig "blog" updated
```

If you need a persistent volume with a particular storage class, you can use the --claim-class option.

When a persistent volume is added to a deployment configuration using oc set volume, the application will be automatically redeployed. The one persistent volume will then be mounted into each container, for all instances of your application. If a pod is restarted, the same persistent volume will be used by the replacement pod. Any changes made in the persistent volume are therefore shared between all instances and will be preserved across restarts of the application.

To list the persistent volumes that have been added against an application, run oc set volume against the deployment configuration without any additional arguments:

```
$ oc set volume dc/blog
deploymentconfigs/blog
  pvc/blog-data (allocated 5GiB) as data
    mounted at /opt/app-root/src/media
```

This will show the actual size of the persistent volume being used. The size may be larger than what was requested, because persistent volumes are defined with set sizes. OpenShift will use the smallest volume size available that satisfies your request. The limit on how much you can store in the persistent volume is dictated by the capacity of the persistent volume and not the size of your request.

To see the current persistent volume claims in a project, run oc get pvc:

```
$ oc get pvc
NAME      STATUS VOLUME CAPACITY ACCESSMODES STORAGECLASS AGE
blog-data Bound  pv0088 5Gi      RWO,ROX,RWX              3m
```

This will also show all the access modes the persistent volume you were allocated supports.

Unmounting a Persistent Volume

To stop using a persistent volume with an application, you can use the `oc set volume --remove` command. You must supply the name used to identify the volume mount in the deployment configuration:

```
$ oc set volume dc/blog --remove --name data
deploymentconfig "blog" updated
```

This command will only remove the volume mount from the container of the application. It does not delete the persistent volume. Running `oc get pvc`, you should still see the persistent volume claim listed.

Reusing a Persistent Volume Claim

If you have a persistent volume claim that you previously unmounted from an application, the `oc set volume --add` command can be used to add it back to the application:

```
$ oc set volume dc/blog --add \
  --claim-name blog-data --name data --mount-path /opt/app-root/src/media
deploymentconfig "blog" updated
```

As the persistent volume claim already exists, you do not need to specify a volume type, the requested size of the volume, or the desired access mode. The name passed to the `--claim-name` option must, though, match that of the existing persistent volume claim.

Sharing Between Applications

If the access mode of a persistent volume is `ReadWriteMany` or `ReadOnlyMany`, you can safely mount that persistent volume against multiple applications at the same time. This will allow you to use a single persistent volume to share data between the applications.

To share one persistent volume between multiple applications but have them be able to see only a subset of what is stored in the persistent volume, you can pass the `--sub-path` option to `oc set volume --add`, specifying a subdirectory of the persistent volume which should be mounted into the container for the application.

Sharing Between Containers

If multiple containers are being run in one pod, they can all share a persistent volume if they need to see the same files. The same files will, though, also be shared with all other pods running the same application.

If the requirement for sharing files is only between the containers in that pod, and files do not need to be persistent across a restart of a pod, a special volume type called emptyDir can be used.

This type of volume is allocated from local storage on each node and is dedicated to the pod. When the pod is restarted, the storage is deleted.

In addition to being able to be used to hold normal files, you can also create special file types such as Unix sockets in the volume, or you can mount the volume at /dev/shm to enable shared memory access. This way, applications in the different containers can communicate with each other.

If you're using init containers, this type of volume can also be used to map files that were generated by the init container into the application container. These could be data files, configuration files, or a customized startup script for the application.

When using oc set volume to add a volume of this type, use the --type=emptyDir option. By default the volume will be mounted against all containers in the pod. If you need to specify a subset of the containers, use the --container option to name them.

Deleting a Persistent Volume

When a persistent volume is unmounted from all applications, the persistent volume claim, along with the persistent volume, will still exist. Any existing data you added to the persistent volume will still be there.

If you no longer need the persistent volume, you can release it by running the oc delete pvc command on the persistent volume claim:

```
$ oc delete pvc/blog-data
persistentvolumeclaim "blog-data" deleted
```

The reclaim policy of a persistent volume will usually be Recycle, meaning that as soon as you delete the persistent volume, its contents will be deleted and the persistent volume will be returned to the pool of available persistent volumes.

To guard against accidental deletion of persistent volumes, a cluster admin can elect to set the reclaim policy on a persistent volume to Retain. In this case if you do accidentally delete a persistent volume, it will not be recycled automatically. If you know this reclaim policy is being used, you can contact your cluster admin to see if you can get the persistent volume claim reinstated with the same persistent volume. You will need to know what the original volume name was for the persistent volume claim. You can get this for a current persistent volume claim from the output of running oc get pvc.

Copying Data to a Volume

If you have your application running and a persistent volume mounted, you can copy a directory from your local system into the persistent volume using oc rsync.

First determine the name of the pod for your application that mounts the persistent volume:

```
$ oc get pods --selector app=blog
NAME            READY    STATUS    RESTARTS    AGE
blog-1-5m3q6    1/1      Running   0           2m
```

You can then run oc rsync to copy the directory.

```
$ oc rsync /tmp/images blog-1-5m3q6:/opt/app-root/src/media --no-perms
```

The --no-perms option tells oc rsync not to attempt to preserve permissions on directories and files. This is necessary, when copying files to the local container file-system, and the directory into which files are being copied is not owned by the user ID the container is running as, but rather by the user that the S2I builder was run as. Without this option, oc rsync would fail when it attempts to change the permissions on the directory.

The oc rsync command can also be used to copy directories or files from a running container back to the local system. Copying in either direction can be run as a one-off event, or you can have oc rsync continually monitor for changes and copy files each time they are changed.

Summary

OpenShift is able to support more than just stateless 12-factor or cloud-native applications. Using the ability to mount persistent volumes into containers, applications can save data that needs to be shared between instances or persist across restarts.

Persistent storage can be claimed based on the specific type or class of storage, and the size of the persistent volume required. OpenShift will mount the persistent volume into a container, and the storage will automatically follow the application, even if the application is moved to a different node in the OpenShift cluster.

## CHAPTER 15

Resource Quotas and Limits

Whenever you interact with OpenShift, you will perform actions as a specific user. If you are deploying applications, your actions will be carried out in the context of a project. You cannot just do anything you like, though. Controls exist around what you can do, as well as how many resources you can consume.

Quotas on resource objects control how many projects you create, how many applications you can deploy, or how many persistent volumes you can use. A quota can also be specified that limits the maximum amount of memory or CPU you can use across all your applications. Limit ranges can further control how you use memory or CPU by dictating how much an individual application can use.

Within any limit ranges defined, you can specify how much memory or CPU an application actually requires. This allows you to partition up your overall memory and CPU quotas to make best use of the available resources to deploy as many different applications or instances as you can. Defining how much memory and CPU your application requires also helps the OpenShift scheduler to work out the best place to run your application.

In this chapter you will learn about the quotas and limits that control how many resources a project and application can consume. You will also learn about how to specify how much memory and CPU your application needs.

What Is Managed by Quotas

Quotas are used to manage two categories of resources.

The first category is resource objects—i.e., how many objects you can create of certain types. A quota on this category of resources might control how many projects you can create, how many applications you are able to deploy, how many instances of your application you can run, or how many persistent volumes you can use.

The second category is compute resources. A quota in this category could set the total amount of CPU and memory resources you have available to use across all your applications.

Quotas on compute resources may be defined depending on the type of workload. A quota on non-terminating resources would be applied to the applications you have permanently running. A quota on terminating resources would be applied to temporary workloads, such as building an image from source code in OpenShift or running a job.

Whether the projects you are working on are subject to resource quotas will depend on how the OpenShift cluster has been configured. There are a couple of ways you can determine whether quotas are being applied to a project.

Quotas and limit ranges are not predefined when you use Minishift or `oc cluster up`. When using these, how much resources you can consume is dictated by the amount of the underlying host has available.

In the web console, you can view any quotas that are being applied to a project, by selecting Quota from the Resources menu in the lefthand navigation bar (Figure 15-1).

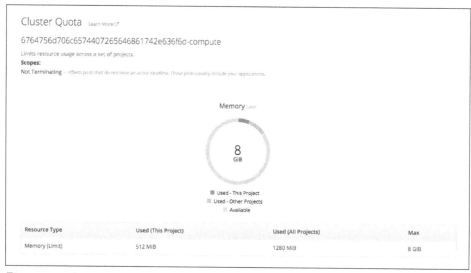

Figure 15-1. Resource quotas

From the command line, how you determine what quotas are being applied will depend on whether they are applied on a per-project basis or across all the projects you create.

When quotas are applied on a per-project basis, you can view them with the `oc describe quota` command. If the quota is across multiple projects, you would instead view them with the `oc describe appliedclusterresourcequota` command.

Any quota that is being applied will have been set up in advance by the cluster admin. As a user, you have no ability to change the quotas through OpenShift.

Because there is a great deal of flexibility in how quotas are defined, different OpenShift clusters may apply them differently. With a typical OpenShift cluster configuration you will see separate quotas for CPU and memory. It is also possible you may see a quota only for memory. This is because a cluster admin can configure the cluster such that CPU is limited in ratio to the amount of memory allocated to the container. Using 1 Gi of memory for a container might translate to 2 CPU cores. Reducing the memory allocated to a container in this scenario to 512 Mi would drop the limit on the amount of CPU available to a single CPU core.

For additional information on this topic, see the OpenShift documentation on over-commitment of resources (*https://docs.openshift.org/latest/admin_guide/overcommit.html*).

Quotas versus Limit Ranges

A *quota* sets an upper bound on the total amount of resources that can be consumed across all your applications. The quota does not determine how many compute resources an individual application can consume when multiple applications are being deployed. The only constraint in that case is that the total compute resources consumed by all applications cannot exceed the quota.

How many compute resources an individual application can consume is controlled by a *limit range*. A limit range is applied on a per-project basis. You can find the limit ranges for a project at the bottom of the *quotas* page in the web console, as shown in Figure 15-2.

The limit range details are at the bottom of the same *quotas* page that shows Cluster Quota, as mentioned in the previous section. Navigate to Resources → Quota in the lefthand menu. Note that the quota page is very long and has other details that aren't shown.

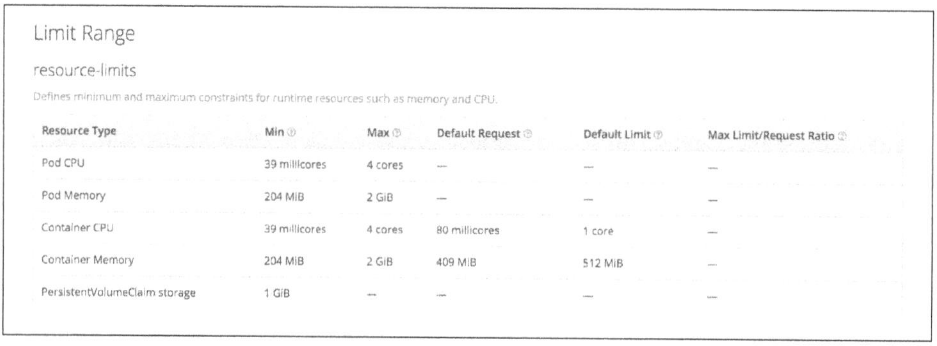

Limit Range

resource-limits

Defines minimum and maximum constraints for runtime resources such as memory and CPU.

Resource Type	Min	Max	Default Request	Default Limit	Max Limit/Request Ratio
Pod CPU	39 millicores	4 cores	—	—	—
Pod Memory	204 MiB	2 GiB	—	—	—
Container CPU	39 millicores	4 cores	80 millicores	1 core	—
Container Memory	204 MiB	2 GiB	409 MiB	512 MiB	—
PersistentVolumeClaim storage	1 GiB	—	—	—	—

Figure 15-2. Limit ranges

The limit ranges can also be viewed from the command line using `oc describe limits`.

If quotas have been defined for memory and CPU usage, limit ranges for those compute resources will also be defined for the project. This is necessary so that when an application doesn't define the amount of memory or CPU it requires, there are default values that can be applied.

Requests Versus Limits

In addition to the definition of the amount of memory and CPU an application requires factoring into quota calculations, it is also a major factor in how the OpenShift scheduler works out where to deploy your application. When the scheduler knows the minimum amount of memory and CPU you require, it can ensure that your application is run on a node where there are enough compute resources available to satisfy your request.

Even if quotas have not been defined, a cluster admin will normally still add limit range definitions to projects. This will ensure that applications will always carry some estimate of the compute resources they require, and the scheduler will be better able to manage the placement of applications onto nodes.

When defining the required compute resources, you can define for each container a request and a limit value for both CPU and memory. The request value indicates the minimum amount of compute resources the application running in the container requires. The limit is the maximum that it can grow to consume.

If a container doesn't specify a request or limit value and a limit range defines a default value for that compute resource, the default value is used.

Based on whether the request and limit values are set and their values, an application will be assigned to a quality-of-service tier. This will affect how the application is dealt with in situations such as when available resources on a node are low. An application marked with a lower quality of service is more likely to be evicted from a node and restarted on a different node, potentially affecting the availability of the application.

For more details on how quotas and limits are applied, including quality-of-service tiers, check out the OpenShift documentation on quotas and limit ranges (*https:// docs.openshift.org/latest/dev_guide/compute_resources.html*).

Resource Requirements

To see the resource limits that are being applied to an application, you can run oc describe on one of the pods for the application. This will show, for each container in the pod, both the request and limit values for CPU and memory:

```
Limits:
  cpu:    500m
  memory: 256Mi
Requests:
  cpu:    40m
  memory: 204Mi
```

These are the values after taking the defined values from the deployment configuration and filling in missing values from the project default limits.

To see what values the deployment configuration had specified, run oc describe on that:

```
Limits:
  memory: 256Mi
```

In this example, only the limit value for memory was specified. As such, the request value was filled in from the project default limits. As CPU resource requirements were not defined, these were also filled in from the project defaults.

To modify the resource requirements for your application, you can run the oc set resources command:

```
$ oc set resources dc/blog --limits memory=512Mi
deploymentconfig "blog" resource requirements updated
```

For a typical OpenShift cluster, you will be able to set request and limit values for both CPU and memory. Any values supplied must lie between the minimum and maximum specified by the limit range for the resource, and the request cannot be greater than the limit.

If you are not provided with a CPU quota, and available CPU is calculated in ratio to memory, you will only be able to set the resource requirements for memory. It is also possible with some OpenShift cluster configurations that any request value will be ignored, with it being calculated as a percentage of the limit. Ask your cluster admin how quotas have been configured, or check their documentation for more details if you're using an OpenShift service provider.

Overriding Build Resources

Limit ranges do not apply to containers run when building images in OpenShift from source. The request and limit values for builds on both CPU and memory are defined globally for the whole cluster. A typical limit on memory for a build would be 512 Mi. This may not be enough when installing some packages as part of an S2I build when using the `nodejs` or `python` S2I builders.

These values for CPU and memory can be overridden, but at the time of writing this book the `oc set resources` command could not be used to update a build configuration. By the time you are reading this, this likely will have changed. To change the limit value for memory on a build configuration you can run:

```
$ oc set resources bc/blog --limits memory=1Gi
buildconfig "blog" resource requirements updated
```

If `oc set resources` doesn't work for the version of OpenShift you are using, you can instead use `oc patch` to update the build configuration:

```
$ oc patch bc/blog --patch '{"spec":{"resources":{"limits":{"memory":"1Gi"}}}}'
buildconfig "blog" patched
```

When setting memory and CPU limits for a build, the values need to be less than the quota for terminating resources.

Summary

When you create a new project to hold your applications, quotas dictate how many CPU and memory resources those applications can use. Separate quotas exist for nonterminating and terminating workloads. The nonterminating quota is what is applied to your applications. The terminating quota is what is applied to builds and jobs.

If you don't state explicitly how many resources your application requires, default values will be applied for requested and maximum resources. Indicating the amount of resources you require is important, as it enables OpenShift to schedule workloads to where resources are available.

## CHAPTER 16

Monitoring Application Health

When you deploy your application, OpenShift needs to know whether it has started up correctly before traffic is sent to it. Even after it has started up, you want it to be restarted if it is not working correctly.

To monitor the health of an application, you can define a *readiness probe* and a *liveness probe*. OpenShift will periodically run the probes to watch over your application.

The readiness probe is used to determine whether your application is in a state where it is okay for other applications or external users to communicate with it. The liveness probe is used to determine whether your application is still running correctly.

In this chapter you will learn more about what each of these probes is for and what actions are taken when they succeed or fail. You will also learn about the different ways you can implement the probes.

The Role of a Readiness Probe

A readiness probe checks whether an application is ready to service requests.

When a new pod is created for your application, if you provide a readiness probe, it will be used to periodically check whether the instance of your application running in that pod is ready to handle requests. When the probe succeeds for the new pod, the IP address for the pod will be added to the list of endpoints associated with the service.

Once the pod's IP address is added to the list of active endpoints, other applications will be able to communicate with it via the IP address or internal hostname of the service. If a route has been created against the service, the routing layer will be reconfigured automatically so that external traffic can reach the application running in the new pod.

If the probe keeps failing when the pod is starting, the deployment of that pod will be deemed to have failed. This will result in the whole deployment or scaling-up event failing.

If the probe is successful and the IP address is added to the endpoints, the probe will still be used periodically to check that the application continues to be able to accept requests. If the probe subsequently starts to fail, the IP address will be removed from the list of endpoints associated with the service, but the pod will be left to run.

This failure of a probe after an application has been successfully started could be used by an application to control where traffic flows in the event that the application queue for handling requests has filled up for that instance. When the backlog of requests has been cleared, the application should again pass the readiness check and the IP address will be added back to the list of endpoints associated with the service.

If no readiness probe is provided, the pod will be assumed to always be ready, with the IP address being added to the list of endpoints associated with the service as soon as the pod is started and only removed if the pod is shut down.

It is recommended that a readiness probe always be used if using the Rolling deployment strategy. This is because it ensures that a new pod will have requests directed to it only when it's ready, ensuring that you have zero downtime when deploying a new version of your application.

The topic of deployment strategies and rolling deployments will be covered in more detail in Chapter 17.

The Role of a Liveness Probe

A liveness probe checks whether an application is still working.

When you provide a liveness probe, it will be used to periodically check whether the instance of your application running in a pod is still running and whether it is also working correctly.

If the probe keeps failing, the pod will be shut down, with a new pod started up to replace it.

Using an HTTP Request

The first mechanism by which a probe can be implemented is using an HTTP GET request. The check is deemed successful if the HTTP response code returned by the application for the request is between 200 and 399.

To register an HTTP request as a probe, run the `oc set probe` command against the deployment configuration. Use the `--readiness` and/or the `--liveness` option, depending on which types of probes you want to set up. Then use the `--get-url` option to provide the URL for the handler implementing the probe:

```
$ oc set probe dc/blog --readiness --get-url=http://:8080/healthz/ready
```

When specifying the URL, leave out the hostname part. The hostname will be automatically filled in with the IP address of the pod that the probe is being used to check. The port number must be specified and should be the port the application running in the pod uses to accept connections for HTTP requests.

Although you could use an existing URL that a web application handles, it is recommended that you create dedicated handlers for each type of probe. This way you can tailor each handler to implement checks specific to the type of probe.

To remove the probes, you can use the `--remove` option to `oc set probe`:

```
$ oc set probe dc/blog --readiness --liveness --remove
```

Using a Container Command

A probe relying on an HTTP request requires that the application be a web application, or that a separate web server be deployed in the same container or in a sidecar container that can handle the request and perform the required checks. An HTTP request would not be suitable for a traditional database.

The next mechanism by which a probe can be implemented is by using a command executed inside the container that is running the application.

This could be any command that could be run at the command line in the container. If the exit status of the command is 0, then the probe will be deemed successful.

To register a container command as a probe, you can run the `oc set probe` command against the deployment configuration. Use the `--readiness` and/or the `--liveness` option, depending on which types of probes you want to set up. Then provide `--` followed by the command to run:

```
$ oc set probe dc/blog --liveness -- powershift image alive
```

It is recommended not to make the command too complicated. Have the command run a script provided with your application and embed any checks within that script. This is because if the details of the check are part of the command—that is, part of the deployment configuration in OpenShift—it will not be versioned along with your application source code if you are using Git.

Using a script in the application source code also makes it easier to change what the check does, without needing to update the deployment configuration at the same time as deploying a new version of your application.

For a database application, the probe script could run a database client command to check whether the database is ready. For a web application, the probe script could check that the web application is okay by making connections against $HOSTNAME: 8080. The $HOSTNAME environment variable will be automatically set for the container to be the hostname for the pod. The port will need to be the one on which the web application is accepting connections for HTTP requests.

If a suitable probe script has not been included in an application image, and the checks required are too complicated to supply in the actual command, a config map could be used to hold a script, with it being mounted into the container via a volume. The command could then execute the script from the volume.

Using a Socket Connection

The final mechanism by which a probe can be implemented is by checking only whether an application accepts a new socket connection. No actual data is sent over the connection. This is suitable only in cases where the application only starts listening for connections if it has started up successfully, and where acceptance of a new connection is enough to indicate the application is running properly.

To register success of a socket connection as a probe, you can run the oc set probe command against the deployment configuration. Use the --readiness and/or the --liveness option, depending on which types of probes you want to set up. Then provide the --open-tcp option with the port as an argument:

```
$ oc set probe dc/blog --readiness --liveness --open-tcp 8080
```

Probe Frequency and Timeouts

To view the details of any readiness or liveness probes, you can run oc describe on the deployment configuration. Details on when the checks are run and tolerance for failures will be displayed:

```
Liveness:   exec [powershift image alive] delay=0s timeout=1s period=10s
            #success=1 #failure=3
Readiness:  http-get http://:8080/healthz/ready delay=0s timeout=1s period=10s
            #success=1 #failure=3
```

The settings for each probe are:

---

delay

How long after a pod has been started, before the first check using the probe is run

timeout

How long the probe is given to respond with a result before it is deemed to have failed

period

How long after a previous check using a probe to wait before the next check is run

#success

The number of successful checks in a row required for the probe to be deemed as having passed

#failure

The number of unsuccessful checks in a row required for the probe to be deemed as having failed

The default settings for these may not be appropriate for all applications.

To override the default settings when adding a probe, additional options can be passed to `oc set probe`.

For example, to set the `delay`, you can use the `--initial-delay-seconds` option:

```
$ oc set probe dc/blog --readiness --get-url=http://:8080/healthz/ready \
  --initial-delay-seconds 10
```

Setting of an initial delay would be required in cases where during startup an application, although it may accept new connections for requests, might not be ready to start handling live requests immediately and will return an HTTP error response until it is ready.

The `timeout` value, which can be overridden by passing the `--timeout-seconds` option, would need to be overridden in cases where the application doesn't always reliably respond with success within the default of one second.

If OpenShift is using `containerd` for running images in containers, the timeout on a probe when using a container command is not implemented. This is due to limitations in the implementation of `containerd` and `docker`. For container commands, it is recommended that the probe script implement its own mechanism for failing a probe after a set time. If this is not done and the probe never returns, the probe will not be failed, nor will subsequent probes be run.

Summary

Health probes enable you to have OpenShift monitor the health of your application. Probes come in two forms, readiness probes and liveness probes.

The readiness probe determines whether an instance of your application is ready to handle traffic and should be included in the list of active instances for your service. When a new instance of your application is started, the readiness probe is also used in initially determining whether the application instance started up correctly and whether a deployment succeeded or failed.

The liveness probe determines whether your application is running okay. If the liveness probe fails for an instance of your application, that instance will be shut down and a new instance created in its place.

## CHAPTER 17

Application Lifecycle Management

When your application is being deployed, scaled up, redeployed, or shut down, it is done following a set of prescribed steps. As you saw in the previous chapter, health probes can be used to determine whether the application successfully starts, is ready to accept requests, and continues to run correctly. These are, though, just part of a larger process dictated by the deployment strategy being used.

OpenShift implements two basic deployment strategies. The default deployment strategy is a *Rolling* deployment. The aim of this deployment strategy is to enable zero-downtime deployments when rolling out an update to an application.

The second deployment strategy is *Recreate*. This is used when you cannot have multiple instances, or versions, of your application running at the same time. It is also necessary to use this deployment strategy when persistent storage is used that can only be bound to a single node in a cluster at a time.

In this chapter you will learn more about these deployment strategies as well as how to define lifecycle hooks, special commands that are executed at set points within a deployment.

You will also learn about hooks that can be associated with the startup and shutdown of individual pods.

Deployment Strategies

A deployment strategy defines the process by which a new version of your application is started and the existing instances shut down.

To view what strategy a deployment is using, run the `oc describe` command on the deployment configuration:

```
Strategy: Rolling
```

The version of OpenShift available at the time of writing this book did not provide a dedicated command to change the deployment strategy. In older versions of Open-Shift you would need to edit the deployment configuration using oc edit, or run oc patch to patch the deployment configuration in place:

```
$ oc patch dc/blog --patch '{"spec":{"strategy":{"type":"Recreate"}}}'
```

A new command, oc set deployment-strategy, is planned for a newer version of OpenShift, which will allow you to set the deployment strategy to Recreate by running:

```
$ oc set deployment-strategy dc/blog --recreate
```

To set the deployment strategy to Rolling with this command, you would use the --rolling option.

Rolling Deployment

A rolling deployment slowly replaces instances of the previous version of an application with instances of the new version of the application. In a rolling deployment a check will be run against a new instance (using the readiness probe) to determine whether it is ready to accept requests, before adding its IP address to the list of service endpoints and scaling down the old instance. If a significant issue occurs, the rolling deployment can be aborted.

This is the default deployment strategy in OpenShift. Because it runs old and new instances of your application in parallel and balances traffic across them as new instances are deployed and old instances shut down, it enables an update with no downtime.

A rolling deployment should not be used in the following scenarios:

- When the new version of the application code will not work with the existing schema of a separate database, and a database migration is required first
- When the new and old application code cannot be run at the same time due to reasons other than dependence on a separate database schema version
- When it wouldn't be safe to run more than one instance of the application at the same time, even of the same version

In these cases the Recreate deployment strategy should be used.

To enable additional actions when a deployment is occurring, you can define two types of lifecycle hooks:

Pre

> This hook is executed before the first new instance of your application is created for the new deployment.

Post

> This hook is executed after all instances of your application for a deployment have been successfully started and the old instances have been shut down.

A container will be created using the new version of the image and the command specified for each hook will be run in it.

An example of a command from a *pre* lifecycle hook would be to enable a database flag to put an application in read-only mode. When the deployment had completed successfully, the *post* lifecycle hook could disable the flag.

In the event that a deployment fails, the *post* lifecycle hook will not be run. In this example, that means the site would remain in read-only mode until a manual action had been taken to work out what failed and the flag disabled.

To add a lifecycle hook, run the `oc set deployment-hook` command on the deployment configuration. Pass the `--pre` or `--post` option to indicate which lifecycle hook should be added. The command should follow `--`:

```
$ oc set deployment-hook dc/blog --pre -- powershift image jobs pre-deployment
```

```
$ oc set deployment-hook dc/blog --post -- powershift image jobs post-deployment
```

By default, no volumes will be mounted into the container the lifecycle hook is run in. To specify volumes to mount from the deployment configuration, use the `--volumes` option and provide the names of the volumes.

Any environment variables specified for the container in the deployment configuration will be passed to the container used to run the hook command. If you need to set additional environment variables just for the hook, use the `--environment` option.

To remove a lifecycle hook, use the `--remove` option:

```
$ set deployment-hook dc/blog --remove --pre --post
```

Recreate Deployment

Instead of starting up new instances of your application while still running old instances, when the Recreate strategy is used, the existing running instances of the application will be shut down first. Only after all the old instances of the application have been shut down will the new instances be started.

This deployment strategy should be used when you cannot run more than one instance of your application at the same time, or when you cannot run instances using old and new code at the same time.

It should also be used in cases where your application uses a persistent volume and the type of the persistent volume is ReadWriteOnce. This is necessary as this type of persistent volume can be attached to only one node in an OpenShift cluster at one time.

 If you are using the Rolling deployment strategy at the same time as using a persistent volume of type *ReadWriteOnce*, resulting in the deployment getting stuck, scale down the number of replicas of your application to zero before switching to a Recreate deployment. Once the application is stopped and the deployment strategy changed, scale the number of replicas back up to one. This will avoid the need to wait for the stuck deployment to time out.

With this strategy, as all old instances of the application will be stopped before deploying instances with the new code, there may be a period of time when your application is not available. Unless you have taken steps to first route traffic to a temporary application that shows a maintenance page, users will see an HTTP 503 Service Unavailable error response.

The *pre* and *post* lifecycle hooks can be defined when using this deployment strategy, along with the following additional hook:

Mid
> This hook is executed after all old instances of your application have been shut down, but before any new instances of your application have been started.

The *mid* hook can be used to safely run any database migrations, as your application will not be running at that point.

To add a *mid* lifecycle hook, run the oc set deployment-hook command on the deployment configuration with the --mid option:

```
$ oc set deployment-hook dc/blog --mid -- powershift image migrate
```

Custom Deployments

In addition to these two basic deployment strategies, various other more complicated strategies can be implemented, including Blue-Green or A/B deployment strategies. These can be implemented by using multiple deployment configurations and reconfiguring which pods for an application are associated with a service or route using labels. Custom strategies like these can be set up manually, or you can provide an image that embeds the logic for handling a deployment and that interacts with Open-

Shift via the REST API to make the changes in resources associated with the application. For further information, check out the OpenShift documentation on deployment strategies (*http://bit.ly/2EHos6t*).

Container Runtime Hooks

The *pre*, *mid*, and *post* hooks are only executed once for each deployment, regardless of the number of replicas of your application you have. They can only be used to run additional actions related to the overall deployment, and not for specific pods.

To perform special actions on each pod, you can define the following hooks:

postStart
> This hook is executed immediately after a container is created. If it fails, the container is terminated and restarted according to its restart policy.

preStop
> This hook is called immediately before a container is shut down. The container is shut down after the hook completes. Regardless of the outcome of the hook, the container will still be shut down.

A *postStart* hook could be used to trigger preloading of data into a cache used by a particular instance of the application. A *preStop* hook could be used as a way to signal a graceful shutdown of the application, allowing more control over how long the application has to finish up current requests.

These hooks can be implemented as a command run within the container for the application or as an HTTP GET request against the application running in the pod, or just the act of creating a socket connection to the application could be used to trigger some action.

The version of OpenShift available at the time of writing this book did not provide a dedicated command to set the container hooks. It is necessary to use `oc edit` on the deployment configuration, or use a JSON-style patch with the `oc patch` command.

To use `oc patch` to set a command to be executed for the *preStop* hook, create a patch file *pre-stop.json* containing:

```
[
  {
    "op": "add",
    "path": "/spec/template/spec/containers/0/lifecycle/preStop/exec/command",
    "value": [ "powershift", "image", "jobs", "graceful-shutdown" ]
  }
]
```

Then run the `oc patch` command, using the patch file as input to the `--patch` option:

```
$ oc patch dc/blog --type=json --patch "`cat pre-stop.json`"
```

The `path` attribute in the patch file indicates what value is being set in the deployment configuration. The `0` after `containers` indicates the first container defined for the deployment configuration. You may need to change this number if there are multiple containers being run in the pod.

Init Containers

Container hooks allow the execution of actions for each instance of a pod, but they can only act on an already running pod, either immediately after startup or prior to shutdown. For the case of wanting to perform an action before the application starts, you can use an *init container*.

Init containers are like regular containers in a pod, except that they run in sequence and must each complete successfully before the next init container is run and finally the application is started. An init container could be used to run a command using the same image used for the application, or could use a different image.

One example of how an init container could be used is to update files in a persistent volume from a directory in the application image, with the persistent volume then being mounted on top of that same directory.

This would allow a persistent volume to be populated with the files from the image, but also allow additional files to be added to the directory, either by the application or manually, which would persist across restarts of the application. The additional files could at a later date be incorporated into the image so they would be available for completely new deployments.

For this use case, you would first mount the persistent volume against the application container:

```
$ oc set volume dc/blog --add \
    --type=pvc --claim-size=1G --claim-mode=ReadWriteOnce \
    --claim-name blog-htdocs --name htdocs --mount-path /opt/app-root/src/htdocs
```

At this point the persistent volume will have hidden the files originally contained in the image where the persistent volume was mounted, and the directory will appear to be empty.

To copy the files from the application image to the persistent volume using an init container, create a patch file called *init-containers.json* containing:

```
[
  {
    "op": "add",
    "path": "/spec/template/spec/initContainers",
    "value": [
      {
        "name": "blog-htdocs-init",
```

```
            "image": "blog",
            "volumeMounts": [
                {
                    "mountPath": "/mnt",
                    "name": "htdocs"
                }
            ],
            "command": [
                "rsync",
                "--archive",
                "--no-perms",
                "--no-times",
                "/opt/app-root/src/htdocs/",
                "/mnt/"
            ]
        }
    ]
  }
]
```

Then run the oc patch command, using the patch file as input to the --patch option:

```
$ oc patch dc/blog --type=json --patch "`cat init-containers.json`"
```

The init container will mount the persistent volume, but it will mount it temporarily on the directory */mnt*. The files can then be copied from the application image to the persistent volume. When the main application container runs, the persistent volume will instead be mounted on the directory from which the files were copied.

One extra command you need to run before you are done is:

```
$ oc set image-lookup dc/blog
```

This is necessary as, unlike with regular containers in the pod, when using init containers including the name of an image stream in the image field doesn't automatically result in the field being resolved against an image stream. The oc set image-lookup command enables local lookup so the name will be resolved against the image stream for the application image.

Summary

Deployment strategies define the process by which a new version of your application is started and the existing instances shut down. The two main deployment strategies are Rolling and Recreate.

In the case of a Rolling deployment, for each instance of your application, a new instance will be started up before the old instance is shut down. This ensures there is always an instance of your application running and no downtime occurs.

For Recreate, all instances of your application will be shut down before any new instances are created. Users of your application will see it as being unavailable for a period as the deployment occurs.

Which deployment strategy can be used is dictated by how your application is implemented and the type of persistent storage the application is using.

Within the overall flow of a deployment, it is possible to define hooks that allow you to run additional actions, before, during, or after a deployment. Additional actions can also be run for each instance of your application.

## CHAPTER 18

Logging, Monitoring, and Debugging

Development and deployment of your application may not always go smoothly. It is therefore important to understand what tools are available in OpenShift for helping you to debug issues.

The primary means of working out what is going on are the logs generated when you build, deploy, and are running your application. These are supplemented by system events generated by OpenShift. You can also monitor for changes to resource objects.

To debug your running application, you can start up an interactive terminal session running inside your application container. For debugging why your application may not be starting up, you can create a special container with your application image where, instead of the application being run automatically, you are given an interactive shell so you can start it up yourself.

In this chapter you will learn about how to access logs, how to interact with your application using an interactive shell, and other methods for monitoring your application.

Viewing the Build Logs

When you build your application from source code in OpenShift, either using an S2I builder or from a `Dockerfile`, the build process is co-ordinated by a build pod. Any log output from the build process will be captured against this build pod.

To view the build logs for the last build run, you can run the `oc logs` command against the build configuration for your application:

```
$ oc logs bc/blog
Receiving source from STDIN as archive ...
Pulling image "registry.access.redhat.com/rhscl/python-35-rhel7@sha256:..." ...
Collecting powershift-cli[image]
```

```
Downloading powershift-cli-1.2.5.tar.gz
....
```

If the build is still running, you can supply the `--follow` option to have the build followed to completion.

To debug the build process itself, you can define the `BUILD_LOGLEVEL` environment variable for the build configuration. This will cause OpenShift to log messages about what it is doing:

```
$ oc set env bc/blog BUILD_LOGLEVEL=9
```

In order to see logs from a prior build, first use `oc get builds` to get a list of the builds, supplying a label selector if you have multiple applications deployed to the same project:

```
$ oc get builds --selector app=blog
NAME      TYPE      FROM        STATUS      STARTED         DURATION
blog-2    Source    Git@9d745d3 Complete    2 minutes ago   59s
blog-1    Source    Git@b6e9504 Complete    5 minutes ago   1m37s
```

You can then run `oc logs` against the specific build:

```
$ oc logs build/blog-1
```

You could also run `oc get pods` to see the list of all pods and run `oc logs` on the build pod:

```
$ oc logs pods/blog-1-build
```

Because OpenShift will clean up old containers and builds, you will not have a full history of builds. For an old build, although the record of the build may still exist, the container and logs may have already been purged, and attempting to view the logs will result in an error.

Viewing Application Logs

To view application logs using `oc logs`, you need to identify the pods for each instance of your application and run `oc logs` on each:

```
$ oc get pods --selector app=blog
NAME            READY   STATUS    RESTARTS   AGE
blog-2-116wg    1/1     Running   0          5m
blog-db-1-1bss8 1/1     Running   0          30m

$ oc logs pod/blog-5-116wg
...
```

You can use the `--follow` option to `oc logs` to continually monitor the logs for that pod.

By default no timestamps are shown for individual log messages unless the application itself adds them. To display alongside logged messages the time of the message as captured by OpenShift, use the `--timestamps` option.

When a new deployment is running, you can view its progress by running `oc logs` on the deployment configuration for the application:

```
$ oc logs --follow dc/blog
--> Scaling blog-2 down to zero
--> Scaling blog-3 to 1 before performing acceptance check
--> Waiting up to 10m0s for pods in rc blog-3 to become ready
--> Success
```

At other times, running `oc logs` on the deployment configuration will result in the logs for the last pod to be created being displayed.

Logs for each pod can also be viewed in the web console, and when aggregated logging has been enabled for the OpenShift cluster by the cluster admin, you can see them all together and perform queries against the logs. For more information, see the OpenShift documentation on configuring aggregated logging (*https://docs.open shift.org/latest/install_config/aggregate_logging.html*).

Monitoring Resource Objects

Whether it be building an image, performing a new deployment, or running the application, all work in OpenShift is typically run in a pod. You can see the list of pods by running `oc get pods`, but this will just be the list of pods in existence at that time. If you want to monitor a set of resource objects over time, you can pass the `--watch` option to `oc get`. This will allow you to watch as pods are created and subsequently terminated:

```
$ oc get pods --watch
NAME          READY STATUS            RESTARTS AGE
blog-3-5jkg0  1/1   Running           0        1m
blog-2-build  0/1   Pending           0        0s
blog-2-build  0/1   ContainerCreating 0        0s
blog-2-build  1/1   Running           0        6s
blog-3-deploy 0/1   Pending           0        0s
blog-3-deploy 0/1   ContainerCreating 0        0s
blog-2-build  0/1   Completed         0        1m
blog-3-deploy 1/1   Running           0        5s
blog-3-5jkg0  1/1   Terminating       0        2m
blog-3-5jkg0  0/1   Terminating       0        2m
blog-4-d6xbx  0/1   Pending           0        0s
blog-4-d6xbx  0/1   ContainerCreating 0        0s
blog-4-d6xbx  0/1   Running           0        8s
blog-4-d6xbx  1/1   Running           0        10s
blog-3-deploy 0/1   Completed         0        32s
blog-3-deploy 0/1   Terminating       0        32s
```

Monitoring System Events

Watching pods can give you a good view of what is changing in the system when a new build and deployment are occurring. You can also see when a pod running an instance of your application is terminated and restarted. What monitoring pods will not tell you is *why* something happened.

Similarly, logs can tell you about what is happening with a build or in your application, including errors, but they don't tell you about errors OpenShift itself may encounter, or why OpenShift is taking particular actions.

To monitor what OpenShift is doing for applications running in your project, you can use `oc get events`, passing the `--watch` option to monitor new events as they occur. There are many types of events that can be generated. These include when new builds are run, and when deployments are run when containers are stopped and started, as well as errors such as failure of probes or exceeding a resource quota with a new deployment.

Viewing Container Metrics

To determine how much of your resource quota you are using, you can use the *Quota* page in the web console. The information here will tell you how much of your allocation you have assigned to applications, but it is not a measure of how many resources an application is actually using.

To determine how much an application is using, metrics charts can be found on the project overview in the web console. This shows average use across all instances of your application (see Figure 18-1).

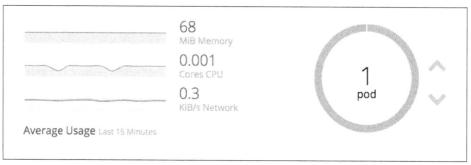

Figure 18-1. Container metrics

Metrics for individual pods can be found on the web console pages for the pods, or under the *Monitoring* page selected from the lefthand navigation bar of the project overview.

Using the knowledge of how much CPU or memory an application is using, you can increase the resource allocation to ensure it has enough resources, or reduce the allocation if it has more than required, allowing you to allocate resources to other applications.

Running an Interactive Shell

Each instance of your application runs in a container, sandboxed off from everything else. The only thing running in the container will be the application processes.

In order to debug what is happening inside the container with your application, you can gain access to the container and run an interactive shell. To do this, run `oc rsh` against the name of the pod:

```
$ oc rsh blog-4-d6xbx
(app-root)sh-4.2$
```

This will work for any container image that includes */bin/sh* within the image. What Unix tools you have access to when debugging your application will depend on what was included in the image.

It is always a good idea to include tools such as `vi`, `curl`, `ps`, and `top` in images to help make it easier to debug an application, check or modify files in the container or an attached persistent volume, or see how much CPU and memory individual processes running in the container are using.

If, rather than an interactive shell, you want to run just a single command that requires no input, use `oc exec`:

```
$ oc exec blog-4-d6xbx env | grep HOSTNAME
HOSTNAME=blog-4-d6xbx
```

Debugging Startup Failures

If your application is failing on startup, with the container also being terminated, OpenShift will keep attempting to restart it. If this keeps happening, the deployment will fail. OpenShift will indicate this by setting the status of the pod to `CrashLoopBack Off`.

To debug a container that will not start you can use the `oc debug` command, running it against the deployment configuration for your application:

```
$ oc debug dc/blog
Debugging with pod/blog-debug, original command:
  container-entrypoint /tmp/scripts/run
Waiting for pod to start ...
Pod IP: 10.131.1.193
```

```
If you don't see a command prompt, try pressing enter.
(app-root)sh-4.2$
```

Rather than starting your application, an interactive shell session will be started. The startup messages when oc debug is run will show what the original command was that would have been run for the container.

From the shell, you can verify any environment variables or configuration files, change them if necessary, and then run the original command to start your application. Any output from your command will be displayed in the terminal so you can see what error may be occurring on startup.

When your application is started with oc debug, it will not be possible to connect to it from any other pods using its service name, nor will it be exposed by a route for your application if one was created. If you need to send it requests, use oc get pods to get the name of the pod created for the debug session, then use oc rsh from a separate terminal to get a second interactive shell in the container. You can then run a command, such as curl, against the application from inside the container:

```
$ oc get pods
NAME              READY    STATUS     RESTARTS    AGE
blog-4-d6xbx      1/1      Running    0           1h
blog-debug        1/1      Running    0           6m

$ oc rsh blog-debug
(app-root)sh-4.2$ curl $HOSTNAME:8080
...
```

Because any persistent volumes defined in the deployment configuration will also be mounted, if you are using a persistent volume type of ReadWriteOnce, you will first need to scale down the application by running oc scale --replicas=0; otherwise, the debug container will not be able to mount the persistent volume at the same time and will fail to start.

Summary

OpenShift captures and logs the output from each instance of your application. To interact directly with an application instance, you can start an interactive terminal session within the container your application is running in. You can use this to check settings of environment variables, look at config files, view the contents of files in mounted persistent volumes, or directly interact with the processes that make up your running application. Details about resources used can be determined using process monitoring tools within the container, or by looking at metrics collected by OpenShift for overall pod usage.

Logs are also available covering the steps run to build an application image and deploy it. You can monitor the progress of a deployment by watching the pods as they are created and destroyed, and by watching events that OpenShift generates about what it is doing and the errors that occur. Errors that occur when your application is started can be investigated by starting a debug session in a special pod started with the same environment as your application, but where an interactive shell is provided rather than starting the application.

Afterword

As OpenShift provides the capabilities of both CaaS and PaaS environments, making it possible to host a large range of different applications, it is hard to choose what should be covered in a book like this. As a developer myself, I have tried to focus on the core features of OpenShift and using it to build and deploy applications.

By focusing on the fundamentals, I hope I have put you in a good position to better understand OpenShift and how you can adapt it to develop and deploy your own applications. Even if you don't find everything in this book immediately relevant to what you are doing now, my goal has been that it will serve as a useful reference you can come back to for help later on.

What Was Covered

The core features of using OpenShift that were covered in this book were:

- Deploying an application from a pre-existing container image for your application

- Building a custom container image using instructions in a `Dockerfile` or from application source code using an S2I builder

- Customizing the build process for constructing a container image, and how you can create your own S2I builder

- Providing configuration and secrets to your application, and how to work with persistent storage

- Making your web application visible to users outside the OpenShift cluster so they can use it

- Controlling the amount of CPU and memory resources your application is able to use

- Monitoring your application to determine whether it starts up correctly and continues to keep running okay

- Strategies available for deploying your application and requirements for being able to perform zero-downtime deployments

- Monitoring your application, and how to access it to debug problems when they occur

Final Words

With each release of OpenShift, the breadth of what it can do keeps growing. This is because of the constant work that is occurring upstream in the Kubernetes project and also in other open source community projects that OpenShift combines with Kubernetes.

If you are interested in contributing to the development of OpenShift, check out the OpenShift Origin (*https://www.openshift.org*) project. If you only want to track what is happening in OpenShift, join the OpenShift Commons (*http://commons.open shift.org*) or subscribe to the OpenShift blog (*https://blog.openshift.com*). These provide regular updates on OpenShift and how people are using it, in the form of webinars, videos, and blog posts.

If you have questions about using OpenShift, you can reach the OpenShift development team through the OpenShift mailing lists (*https://lists.openshift.redhat.com/ openshiftmm/listinfo*), or in the `#openshift-dev` channel on IRC's Freenode network. Community support for OpenShift Online can be found on Google Groups (*https:// groups.google.com/d/forum/openshift*) or Stack Overflow (*http://stackoverflow.com*).

Index

Symbols

#openshift-dev channel, 138

A

A/B deployment, 124
access modes, 104
access tokens, 16
acknowledgments, xiii
admin role, 23
application example
    playground environments, 6
    source code for, 6
application logs, 130
applications
    adding to projects, 19-28
    building from source, 41-49, 51-56
    deleting, 34
    deploying from images, 29-32
    deploying from source, 41-49, 51-56
    deploying using web console, 34-36
    deployment overview, 5
    images and security, 38
    importing images, 36
    lifecycle management for, 121-128
    monitoring health of, 115-120
    pushing to the registry, 37
    runtime configuration, 33
    scaling up, 33
    updating builder image, 45
    viewing in web console, 32
assemble scripts, overriding, 66

B

base64 encoding, 90

binary input builds, 46
Blue-Green deployment, 124
build artifacts
    extracting and saving, 75
    restoring, 75
build strategies (see also docker build strategy;
    source build strategy, Source-to-Image)
    custom, 42
    docker, 51-56
    overview of, 41
    pipeline, 42
    source, 42-49
    speeding up build times, 73-78
buildconfig, 43
builder scripts, overriding, 66
builds logs, 129

C

caching, 73
catalog
    adding S2I builders to, 63
    deploying from, 24-26
CentOS, 1
chained builds, 77
cloud computing
    Containers as a Service (CaaS), 4, 38
    Platform as a Service (PaaS), 2, 4, 49, 56, 64,
        83
    service models, 2
Cloud Native Computing Foundation (CNCF),
    ix, 4
clusters
    accessing, 13-18
    running, 7-11

CNAME records, 97
code repositories, read-only, 68
collaborators, adding, 22
command-line tool, 14-17
comments and questions, xiii
compute resources
    controlling with limit ranges, 111
    managing with quotas, 110
configmap resource type, 87, 91
configuration
    approaches to, 33
    binary input builds, 46
    config maps, 87
    deleting config maps and secrets, 91
    Docker build strategy, 53-55
    passing environment variables, 85-87
    secrets, 89
    Source build strategy, 48
    storing settings, 85
    working with configuration files, 87-89
containers
    container runtime hooks, 125
    debugging startup failures, 133
    history of, 2
    init containers, 126
    Kubernetes platform and, ix, 4, 38, 49, 83
    orchestrating at scale, 3
    Platform as a Service (PaaS), 4
    pods and, 93
    role of, 2
    viewing container metrics, 132
Containers as a Service (CaaS), 4, 38
CrashLoopBackOff status, 133
custom build strategy, 41

D

data, copying to volumes, 108 (see also persis-
    tent storage)
debugging
    build process, 130
    exposing a pod, 100
    interactive shells for, 129, 133-134
    startup failures, 133
deployment
    custom, 124
    Docker build strategy, 53
    from source, 41-49
    from the catalog, 24-26
    main methods of, 23

of a set of resources, 27
of existing container images, 26, 29-39
overview of, 5, 19, 127
re-create deployment strategy, 123
rolling deployment strategy, 116, 122
strategies for, 121
using web console, 34-36
deploymentconfig, 30, 31
docker build strategy
    defined, 41
    security issues, 52
Docker build strategy
    benefits and drawbacks of, 57
    build and runtime configuration, 53-55
    creating builds, 52
    deploying images, 53
    overview of, 51
    using inline Dockerfiles, 55
docker daemon, 52
Docker Hub, 29
docker tool, 3
Dockerfiles, 5, 51, 55
dotCloud, 3

E

edge termination, 98
edit role, 23
emptyDir volume type, 107
end-to-end integration tests, 48
endpoints, 95
environment variables
    customizing S2I builds with, 65
    passing, 85-87
error code 503 (Service Unavailable), 124
external ports, 99
external routes, 96

F

Fedora, 1
Freenode network, 138
fully qualified hostnames, 96

G

generic webhooks, 83
Git repositories
    accessing private, 80
    adding webhooks, 82
    automating builds using, 5, 79

customizing build triggers, 83

H

health probes, 120 (see also monitors of appli-
cation health)
HomeBrew, 8
hooks
    container runtime hooks, 125
    lifecycle hooks, 122
    mid lifecycle hooks, 124
    post lifecycle hooks, 123
    post-commit hooks, 48
    postStart hooks, 125
    pre lifecycle hooks, 123
    preStop hooks, 125
    webhooks, 82
HTTP 503 Service Unavailable, 124
HTTP protocol, 98-101, 116

I

Image Specification (image-spec), 3
images
    building from Dockerfiles, 51-56
    customizing, 55
    deploying your first, 29-32
    importing, 36
    overriding run script, 68
    pushing to the registry, 37
    security issues, 38
    testing container images, 47
    updating image metadata, 69-71
imagestream, 30
incremental builds, 74, 76
Infrastructure as a Service (IaaS), 2
init containers, 126
integration tests, 48
interactive shells, 133
internal image registry, 37
internal ports, 99
IP addresses, 94-96, 115

K

Katacoda, x
Kubernetes platform, ix, 3, 38, 49, 83

L

life cycle hooks
    webhooks, 82

lifecycle hooks
    container runtime hooks, 125
    mid lifecycle hooks, 124
    post lifecycle hooks, 123
    post-commit hooks, 48
    postStart hooks, 125
    pre lifecycle hooks, 123
    preStop hooks, 125
    purpose of, 122
lifecycle management
    container runtime hooks, 125
    custom deployments, 124
    deployment strategies, 121
    init containers, 126
    overview of, 121, 127
    re-create deployment, 123
    rolling deployment, 122
limit ranges, 111
Linux Container project (LXC), 2
liveness probes, 116 (see also monitors of application health)
local filesystems, 46, 103
local interprocess communication (IPC), 94
local port forwarding, 100
localhost, 94
logging and monitoring (see also monitors of
application health)
    debugging startup failures, 133
    monitoring resources objects, 131
    monitoring system events, 132
    overview of, 129, 134
    running an interactive shell, 133
    viewing application logs, 130
    viewing builds logs, 129
    viewing container metrics, 132

M

metadata, updating, 69-71
mid lifecycle hooks, 124
Minishift, x, 8-11
monitors of application health (see also logging
and monitoring)
    liveness probes, 116
    overview of, 115, 120
    probe frequency and timeouts, 118
    readiness probes, 115
    using container commands, 117
    using HTTP requests, 116
    using socket connections, 118

multitenant network overlay, 96

N

name aliases, 30
networking
    connecting between projects, 96
    containers and pods, 93
    creating external routes, 96
    exposing non-HTTP services, 100
    internal and external ports, 99
    local port forwarding, 100
    multitenant network overlay, 96
    overview of, 93, 101
    services and end points, 94-96
    using secure connections, 98
non-HTTP services, 100
non-standard ports, 100

O

obfuscated values, 90
oc adm pod-network command, 96
oc adm policy command, 23
oc cluster down command, 11
oc cluster up --help command, 11
oc cluster up command, 10, 20
oc command-line tool, 14-17
oc create configmap command, 87
oc create imagestream command, 37
oc create route command, 98
oc create secret generic command, 90
oc debug command, 133
oc delete all command, 92
oc delete command, 34
oc delete pvc command, 107
oc describe appliedclusterresourcequota command, 111
oc describe command, 82, 83, 113, 121
oc describe limits, 112
oc describe pod command, 94
oc describe quota command, 111
oc expose command, 30
oc expose service command, 96
oc expose svc command, 43
oc get -o json command, 87
oc get all command, 31
oc get builds command, 130
oc get command, 30
oc get endpoints command, 95
oc get events command, 132

oc get imagestreams command, 26
oc get is command, 36
oc get pods command, 31, 94, 100, 130
oc get pods,services command, 95
oc get pvc command, 105
oc get rolebindings command, 23
oc get routes command, 32, 43
oc get templates command, 22, 25
oc help command, 17
oc import-image command, 36
oc label command, 91
oc login --help command, 17
oc login command, 16
oc logs -f bc command, 43
oc logs command, 129
oc new-app --name command, 42
oc new-app -L command, 26
oc new-app -S command, 26
oc new-app command, 30, 44, 52, 53
oc new-build command, 44, 53
oc new-project command, 22
oc options command, 17
oc patch command, 125
oc port-forward command, 100
oc projects command, 22
oc rsh command, 94, 133
oc rsync command, 69, 108
oc scale command, 33
oc set build-hook command, 48
oc set deployment-hook command, 123
oc set deployment-strategy, 122
oc set env --list command, 33, 88
oc set env command, 33, 86
oc set probe command, 117
oc set resources command, 113
oc set triggers command, 83
oc set volume --add command, 105
oc set volume --remove command, 106
oc start-build command, 45, 46
oc status command, 31
oc types command, 30
oc whoami --show-server command, 11
oc whoami --show-token command, 17
oc whoami command, 23
online resources, x, 138
Open Container Initiative (OCI), ix, 3
OpenShift
    application deployment, 5
    benefits of, ix, 28, 137

documentation, x
enterprise products, xi
installing and running, 7-11
online resources, x, 138
overview of, ix, 1
product releases, xi
source code for, x
topics covered, ix-x, 5, 137
OpenShift blog, xi, 138
OpenShift Commons, xi, 138
OpenShift Container Platform, xi, 8
OpenShift Dedicated, 7
OpenShift Interactive Learning Portal, 6
OpenShift Online, xi, 7, 37
OpenShift Origin, x, 8, 10, 138
OpenShift REST API, 17
orchestration layer, 3

P

passthrough connection, 98
patches, 45
persistent storage
    access modes for, 104
    claiming persistent volumes, 105
    copying data to volumes, 108
    deleting persistent volumes, 107
    overview of, 103
    re-create deployment and, 124
    reusing persistent volume claims, 106
    sharing between applications, 106
    sharing between containers, 107
    types of, 103
    unmounting persistent volumes, 106
pipeline build strategy, 41
Platform as a Service (PaaS), 2, 4, 49, 56, 64, 83
playground environments, 6
pod resource objects, 31
pods
    connecting to, 94
    container runtime hooks, 125
    exposing, 100
    metrics for, 132
    monitoring over time, 131
    overview of, 93
    readiness probes and, 115
    services and end points, 94-96
    sharing persistent volumes within, 107
ports
    internal and external, 99

local port forwarding, 100
    non-standard, 100
POSIX shared memory, 94
post lifecycle hooks, 123
post-commit hook, 48
postStart hooks, 125
pre lifecycle hooks, 123
preStop hooks, 125
probes, 115-116
projects
    adding collaborators to, 22
    connecting between, 96
    creating, 20-22
    deploying applications, 23-26
    deploying images, 26
    deploying resources, 27
    role of, 19

Q

qualified hostnames, 96
questions and comments, xiii
quotas, 109-114
    overriding for builds, 114
    overview of, 114
    requests vs. limits, 112
    resource quotas vs. limit ranges, 111
    types of, 109
    viewing and modifying resource limits, 113

R

re-create deployment strategy, 123
re-encrypting traffic, 98
readiness probes, 115 (see also monitors of
    application health)
ReadOnlyMany (ROX), 104
ReadWriteMany (RWX), 104
ReadWriteOnce (RWO), 104, 124
Red Hat Container Development Kit, xi, 10
Red Hat Developers program, xi
Red Hat Enterprise Linux (RHEL), 1
replicationcontroller, 31
resource objects
    monitoring, 131
    pod resource objects, 31
    quota restrictions, 109
    service resource objects, 95
resource quotas, 109-114
    overriding for builds, 114
    overview of, 109, 114

quotas vs. limit ranges, 111
requests vs. limits, 112
types of, 109
viewing and modifying resource limits, 113
resources, online, x, 138
REST API endpoints, 17
rolling deployment strategy, 116, 122
root users, 38, 52, 99
routes
    creating external, 96
    secured, 98
run scripts, overriding, 66, 68
runtime images, overriding, 68
Runtime Specification (runtime-spec), 3

S

save-artifacts script, 75
scaling, 3, 33
secret information, 85, 89-92
security issues
    docker build strategy, 52
    sandbox environments, 38
    secret information, 85, 89-92
    using secure connections, 98
Security-Enhanced Linux (SELinux), ix
Server Name Identification (SNI), 98, 100
service, 30
service resource objects, 95
services, exposing, 96
shared memory access, 107
socket connections, 118
Software as a Service (SaaS), 2
Source build strategy
    binary input builds, 46
    build and runtime configuration, 48
    building from local source, 46
    creating separate builds, 44
    defined, 41
    deploying from source, 42
    overview of, 42
    testing container images, 47
    triggering new builds, 45
source code
    assembling for S2I builds, 59
    building applications from, 5, 41-49
    for OpenShift, x
    sample application, 6
Source-to-Image (S2I)
    adding S2I builders to the catalog, 63

assembling source code, 59
benefits and drawbacks of, 51
building application images, 58
building S2I builder images, 62
creating S2I builder images, 60-62
customizing S2I builds, 65-71
list of pre-installed builders, 25
overriding S2I build scripts, 66
overview of, 57, 64
Source build strategy and, 42
speeding up build times, 73-78
using with OpenShift, 62
SSL certificates, 98
storage classes, 103 (see also persistent storage)
system events, monitoring, 132
SystemV semaphores, 94

T

temporary file-storage facilities (tmpfs), 90
timestamps on log messages, 131
triggers
    image change, 45
    tracking source code changes with, 46
typographical conventions, xii

U

Unix root users, 38, 52, 99
updates, 45, 122
user-defined HTTP callbacks, 82

V

versioned source code repositories, 85
view role, 23
virtual machines (VMs), 8

W

web console
    Add to Project button, 25, 34
    adding S2I builders to the catalog, 63
    container metrics, 132
    Deploy Image tab, 26, 35
    deployment using, 34-36
    Import YAML/JSON tab, 27
    interacting with, 13
    Monitoring pages, 132
    New Project button, 20
    project list, 21
    resource quotas, 110

viewing applications in, 32
viewing defined quotas, 110
viewing limit ranges, 112

webhooks, 82-83
workflow, automating, 41, 79-84

About the Author

Graham Dumpleton is a Developer Advocate for OpenShift at Red Hat. Graham is an active member of the Python software developer community and is the author of mod_wsgi, a popular module for hosting Python web applications in conjunction with the Apache HTTPD web server. He also has a keen interest in Docker and Platform as a Service (PaaS) technologies.

Colophon

The animal on the cover of *Deploying to OpenShift* is the sulphur-crested cockatoo (*Cacatua galerita*).

The sulphur-crested cockatoo grows to a length of 44–55 cm (17.5–21.5 in); Australian subspecies are larger than those from New Guinea. The crested cockatoo's plumage is white with yellow-tinged underwings and tails and yellow crests. Their bills are black, and they have grey legs.

This large white cockatoo is often found in wooded habitats of Australia, New Guinea, and the Indonesian islands. The sulphur-crested cockatoo is often considered a pest because of its large numbers in suburban habitats and its loud and raucous call. They are also known to damage fruit and cereal crops, newly planted seedlings, or soft timber. These birds are considered very intelligent and curious. They can live up to 70 years in captivity and 20–40 years in the wild. Unlike most birds, they produce a fine powder to waterproof themselves rather than oil, and they are known to eat clay to detoxify their food, also known as geophagy.

Many of the animals on O'Reilly covers are endangered; all of them are important to the world. To learn more about how you can help, go to *animals.oreilly.com*.

The cover image is from *English Cyclopedia*. The cover fonts are URW Typewriter and Guardian Sans. The text font is Adobe Minion Pro; the heading font is Adobe Myriad Condensed; and the code font is Dalton Maag's Ubuntu Mono.

Learn from experts.
Find the answers you need.

Sign up for a **10-day free trial** to get **unlimited access** to all of the content on Safari, including Learning Paths, interactive tutorials, and curated playlists that draw from thousands of ebooks and training videos on a wide range of topics, including data, design, DevOps, management, business—and much more.

Start your free trial at:

oreilly.com/safari

(No credit card required.)